LEARNING RESOURCE CENTERS IN COMMUNITY COLLEGES

A SURVEY OF BUDGETS AND SERVICES

Sarah Katharine Thomson

American Library Association
Chicago

This survey was funded, in part, by a
deeply appreciated fellowship from
the Council on Library Resources.

Library of Congress Cataloging in Publication Data

Thomson, Sarah Katharine, 1928-
Learning resource centers in community colleges.

1. Municipal university and college libraries--
Administration. 2. Instructional materials centers--
Administration. I. Title.
Z675.M93T52 025.1 75-16150
ISBN 0-8389-0206-5

Printed in the United States of America
Second Printing, January 1976

CONTENTS

PREFACE

In the fall of 1973, Bergen Community College, Paramus, New Jersey, granted a semester's sabbatical leave from the position as Chairman of the Library and Learning Resource Center, and the Council on Library Resources awarded a travel and expense fellowship to study the application of modern techinques of management in community college library learning resource centers. The purpose of this sabbatical and grant was to focus on several outstanding learning resource centers in order to investigate improved skills in administration. Over a period of five weeks, visits were planned to fifteen outstanding community college library learning resource centers in California, Florida, Illinois, Texas, and Virginia/Maryland.

The study was to include several modern techniques of management: personnel management operations research, statistical analysis, PERT analysis, decision theory, queuing theory, inventory theory, and learning theory. When it was completed, the survey would have analyzed the application of these management techniques to the operation of a variety of library learning resource centers.

It became obvious early in the development of the research, however, that no one or group of these techniques was yet being applied (at least, not in a deliberate, data-controlled manner) in enough community college learning resource centers to permit a meaningful normative survey of the type proposed. The most commonly used management technique was Management by Objectives, but even this tool was being used in fewer than half of the learning resource centers.

Therefore, as indicated in the first preliminary report to the Council on Library Resources, dated November 15, 1973, the technique around which the study refocused was a modern management instrument of control -- the budget. Budgetary control had universal application and far-reaching ramifications for the community college learning resource centers. Budgetary decisions affected the plans, policies and objectives of the institutions. Moreover, the various proportions of expenditures directly influenced both the services offered by the learning resource centers and the type and quantity of utilization of the resources.

As the study and the statistics began to evolve, several meaningful comparisons began to emerge. Perhaps these comparisons will help to develop even more outstanding community college learning resource centers in the future.

ACKNOWLEDGEMENTS

I am grateful to Dr. Sidney Silverman, President, and the Trustees of Bergen Community College, Paramus, New Jersey, for a semester's sabbatical leave for the study of the administration of community college learning resource centers. This leave came after six intensive years spent in the establishment, development, planning and building, accreditation, and the move to permanent quarters of the Library and Learning Resources Department of Bergen Community College. The leave provided a much needed opportunity to look extensively at what was being done in other community colleges around the country, to gain new perspective, and to evaluate the barrage of new techniques for learning being explored and developed everywhere.

This project was one of thirty-one selected by the Council on Library Resources for fellowship awards in 1973-74. The fellowship covered expenses of travel, supplies, and report preparation. This report was prepared for the Council on the findings of the project. The assistance of the Council is deeply appreciated.

The design of the study benefitted by the advisement of Dr. Ernest R. DeProspo, Jr., Professor of Library Science of the Rutgers University Graduate School of Library Service. In major and minor ways his suggestions were always beneficial, and his suggestions for approaches to interviewing and comparative methods of data gathering and analysis were invaluable. Preliminary design of the project grew out of the course in administration of learning resource centers in community colleges team taught by Dr. DeProspo, Robert L. Goldberg, and Dorothy F. Deininger.

The selection of the institutions for surveying and the refining of the sample frame benefitted greatly from the extraordinary assistance provided by Dr. Frank L. Schick and the staff of the Library Surveys Branch of the U. S. Office of Education in providing a variety of institutional data on community colleges. Discussions with Dr. Schick on the realities, weaknesses, and problems of measuring library services and utilizing libraries' statistics were very valuable.

This report benefitted beyond measure from the encouragement, suggestions, enthusiasm, and editorial assistance of Mary Patricia Robertson. I thank Barbara Dirr, Catherine Khouri, Faith Moneypenny, Mary O'Malley, Patricia Pflugh, Sharon Schneider, and Susan Thomsen who keypunched, helped assemble data, and typed the manuscript. John Havel designed the cover and the map. The reproduction of the report was done by Richard McDonald and the staff of the Bergen Community College Duplicating Center; their expertise, care, and diligence are very much appreciated.

To the staff of the Library and Learning Resources Department, particularly to Peter Anton Helff, I am deeply grateful for support, assistance, encouragement, and for doing a superb job of minding the shop while I was away.

My prime debt, of course, is to the 137 staff members of the twenty-seven campus learning resource departments I visited during seven weeks of travel in November 1973 through February 1974. They were unfailingly gracious, kind, helpful, generous with varieties of insights, frank and very enlightening. To all of them I am indebted more than I can ever repay. A full list of the campuses visited and people interviewed is included here as Table 1.

TABLE I

CAMPUSES SURVEYED AND STAFF INTERVIEWED

CALIFORNIA

Fullerton College — Fullerton, CA

Shirley E. Bosen, Head Librarian
Derk Gephers, Audio-Visual

Long Beach City College — Long Beach, CA

John E. Geyer, Head Librarian
David Pibel, Reference
Joy Proust, Reference and Circulation
Bobbie J. Smith, Audio-Visual
Vida E. Snow, Acquisitions

Los Angeles City College — Los Angeles, CA

Marian Cushman, Reference Librarian
Robert Gates, Learning Resource Center
Betty Jacobs, Media Production Service
John Nomland, Acting Coordinator
Ronald Pierce, Audio-Visual Center

Mt. San Antonio College — Walnut, CA

Catherine Beamer, Reference
Paul Britz, Study Skills Center
Robert Dobis, Production
Harriette Genung, Dean of Library & Audio-Visual Services
Rita Gurnee, Reference
Eloise Mays, Study Skills Center
Roger McFarland, Audio Visual Services
Susan Puck, Study Skills Center
Charles Varnes, Technical Services & Circulation
David Vredenberg, A-V equipment, Engineering Maintenance

FLORIDA

Broward Community College — Fort Lauderdale, FL

Frances Brown, Head of Public Services
Isaac S. Call, Director of Learning Resources
Gladys Drake, Director of the Library
Eleanor Leary, Periodicals

TABLE I (Continued)

FLORIDA (Continued)

Miami-Dade Community College Miami, FL

District Office

Franklin G. Bouwsma, Vice President, Instructional Services
Virginia Gentle, TV College (Open College)
Sally A. Ream, Central Technical Processing

Downtown Campus

Althea Jenkins, Librarian

North Campus

Claribel Baskin, Library Readers' Services
Kenneth Carbonel, Production
Eleanor Eyman, Director, North Campus Library
Mabel Fletcher, Library Acquisitions
Edith Kastens, Periodicals
Orrin S. Whitten, Instructional Resources Coordinator

South Campus

Jo E. Dewar, Director, South Campus Library
Oral P. Kidder, Instructional Resources Coordinator

Palm Beach Junior College Lake Worth, FL

Margaret Brown, Reference
Wiley C. Douglass, Director, Library Learning Resources Center
Hal D. Foster, Jr. Circulation and Readers Advisor
Ivor Wetherby, Periodicals
Benjamin S. Roberts, Faculty Services Librarian
Milton Thomas, A-V Coordinator

ILLINOIS

College of DuPage Glen Ellyn, IL

Richard L. Ducote, Dean of Learning Resources
Lucile Edwards, Utilization Consultant
Robert Geyer, Director, Materials Utilization & Production
Wayne Stuetzer, Design & Graphics
Robert Veihman, Director, Technical Processes and Materials Distribution

TABLE I (Continued)

ILLINOIS (Continued)

Triton College — Rover Grove, IL

Catherine Campbell, Reference
Joseph Chambers, Audio-Visual Supervisor
Michael Gallager, Multimedia Production
Frederick Gaskin, Dean, Learning Resources Center
Julia Sanger, Circulation
Eugene Westphal, Library Director

William Rainey Harper College — Palatine, IL

Alfred Dunikoski, Graphics
Ambrose Easterly, Director of Processing Services
Peter Vander Haeghen, TV Production
Calvin Stockman, Director, Resources Services
Robert Thieda, Resource Circulation Supervisor
George Voegel, Dean of Learning Resources Center

MARYLAND

Community College of Baltimore — Baltimore, MD

Katherine M. Bruheck, Head Librarian
Clarence Gregory, Director, Learning Resources
Minnie B. Hoch, Reference
Nancy K. Manuel, Circulation
Arthur G. Minderlein, Computer Coordinator

Montgomery College — Rockville, MD

Rockville Campus

Marian Flinchum, Readers' Services
George W. Hathaway, Reference
Robert King, Chairman of Learning Resources
Jessie Meyers, Director of Educational Resources
Edward P. Owens, Chairman of the Library Department

Prince George's Community College — Largo, MD

Alan Mickelson, Materials Design & Production
Leah K. Nekritz, Director of Learning Resources
John Oliva, Selection, Cataloging & Reference
Ronald H. Powell, Reference
David Shore, Associate Dean, Instructional Development
Charmaine S. Yochim, Technical Services & Acquisitions

TABLE I (Continued)

MISSOURI

Junior College District of St. Louis

District Office — St. Louis, MO

Grant MacLaren, Coordinator
Michael Summers, Administrative Associate, Business Services

Florissant Valley Community College — Ferguson, MO

Betty Duvall, Associate Dean, Instructional Resources
Charles Rock, Media Services
Sandy Willenbrink, Administrative Associate

Forest Park Community College — St. Louis, MO

Jacqueline Beulick, Instructional Television
Jo Ellen Flagg, Library
Merce Thornberry, Audio-Visual

Meramac Community College — Kirkwood, MO

Barbara Chesman, Self-Instruction
Virginia Hagebush, Assistant Dean
Abdul Samad, Audio-Visual

NEW JERSEY

Brookdale Community College — Lincroft, NJ

Robert Blumer, Instructional Technology
Peter Bouchard, Audio
Charles Burton, Instructional Development Laboratory
Henry Cody, Media Specialists
Anita Davenport, Media Specialists
Wesley Hutchison, Computer Coordinator
Roy Marks, Director
JoAnn Murphy, Photography
Maria Palumbo, Graphics
Susan Rosenberg, Media Specialist
Joyce Semonev, Circulation

Essex County College — Newark, NJ

John Carmichael, Dean of Instructional Resources
Irving Fitzig, Instructional Media, Production
Zenon Sheparovych, Director of the Library
Robert Spellman, Associate Dean for Instructional Development
Robert Stansbury, Head of Reader Services

TABLE I (Continued)

NEW JERSEY (Continued)

Middlesex County College — Edison, NJ

Edwin M. Ashley, Director, Division of Learning Resources
Herbert H. Hill, Instructional Media
Grace V. LeRoy, Graphics
Jane Posselt, Library Director

OHIO

Cuyahoga Community College

District Office — Cleveland, OH

Albert Jones, Controller
James I. Richey, Director, District Technical Services, Eastern Library
Richard Romoser, Director, Institutional Research & Planning

Eastern Campus — Cleveland, OH

Kenneth Urvan, Instructional Media Services Supervisor

Metropolitan Campus — Cleveland, OH

Derrill C. Dalby, Asst. to Director of Educational Media Center
Russell Duino, Director of the Library
Michael King, Systems Analyst, Computer Center

TEXAS

Dallas County Community College District

Eastfield College — Mesquite, TX

Lawrence N. Di Pietro, Associate Director
Cynthia Gaudian, Coordinator Distribution Services
David McCoy, Asst. Director, Classroom Resources
Nancy Miller, Asst. Director, Instructional Services
William F. Tucker, Director Learning Resources Center
Tom Wilkinson, Center for Independent Study

TABLE I (Continued)

TEXAS (Continued)

Tarrant County Junior College

Northeast Campus — Hurst, TX

Dan C. Echols, Jr., Associate Dean Learning Resources; Director of Instructional Media Services
Tommy Ozburn, Director of Libraries
Kay Stansbery, Coordinator, District Processing Center
Larry Wilson, Asst. Director of Instructional Media

South Campus — Fort Worth, TX

Mary Davidson, Coordinator, TV programs
Frances Law, Coordinator, Graphics & Audio Productions
John Lolley, Director of the Library
Paul Vagt, Dean of Learning Resources
Gaston Walker, Asst. Director, Instructional Media Services, Distribution & Maintenance

VIRGINIA

Northern Virginia Community College

Annandale Campus — Annandale, VA

William Belmore, Coordinator of Learning Laboratory
Joseph Pennell, Coordinator of A-V Services
Lois H. Smith, Coordinator of Library Services

Chapter 1

BACKGROUND AND METHODOLOGY

This study represented a survey of the interrelationship between expenditures and service programs for learning resources in large public community colleges in the United States.

The community colleges in the United States at the time of this study (1973-74) represented a unique and dynamic educational concept. The community college movement, developing since 1946, with its flexibility, open admissions, community liason, and diversified programs has grown to represent almost half of the total entering college population.

Nestled within this exciting educational concept, another phenomenon came into being -- the Learning Resource Center. Known by various names, and directed by various organizational patterns and philosophies, the Learning Resource Centers were nevertheless remarkably similar in one respect: their emphasis on concern for the learner, and their support of the teaching-learning process. That support, however, was developed in a number of diversified approaches, as evidenced by the single most empirical measure of philosophy and policy -- the budget.

Community Colleges included here are all "comprehensive" community colleges, a term indicating that they include in their programs all of the following:

1. Two-year college or university parallel offerings that prepare

students for transfer to four-year baccalaureate programs.

2. Full time transferable and non-transferable career training, usually in occupational curricula in response to local needs.
3. Part-time opportunities for employed persons to upgrade their job skills or retrain for new careers.
4. Courses in general education for adults who want to know more about themselves and their world.
5. Community service programs, of a wide variety of kinds, including concerts, lectures, art exhibits, and short non-credit courses in topics of local interest from agriculture to women's lib.

The term "learning resources" will be used in this study as a collective, comprehensive term meaning all of the library, audiovisual, instructional development, and production personnel and facilities, and all of the instructional content materials, both print and non-print, available on each campus, regardless of location or organizational pattern.

Its essential components, which might be combined in a variety of ways, were:

1. Conventional library services (largely print) including selection and acquisition of a wide variety of materials usually classified by subject, or at least providing by catalog for a subject approach, oriented primarily for service to individuals, and providing distribution, retrieval, and storage. Guidance, advisement, and instruction were an essential part of this service.
2. Media Services (largely audiovisual, or non-print) including

both classroom applications, small group usage, and individual study, both self-directed and instructor monitored. Also included under this category were supply and support functions in both software (content materials) and hardware, engineering and maintenance, and some utilization advisement for both faculty and students. Facilities for utilization of these media resources embraced a variety of forms, from conventional library settings with wet carrels, to highly sophisticated learning laboratories designed to meet the special needs of a particular curriculum. Those learning laboratories varied greatly, from fields such as dental hygiene or language therapy, in environments appropriate to the needs of the learner; some had highly structured packaged learning modules, with detailed instructional objectives, while others supported minimally or undirected activity. Resources were often provided for use outside the campus at the convenience of the individual student.

3. <u>Production of instructional materials</u>, where not commercially available, in a wide variety of formats, including audio, video, graphics, photography, and cinematography.
4. <u>Instructional development assistance and advisement to faculty</u> in clarification of learning objectives, analysis of the components of a learning system, idea design and presentation, engineering of appropriate learning models to meet individual and group learning needs, and evaluation of effectiveness of instruction.

In many community colleges these functions were the responsibility of several different departments, which might or might not have been coordinated; in some community colleges one or more of these functions might not be performed to any significant extent.

Staff responsible for learning resources seemed to have become significantly more involved in the instructional program of community colleges than staff in traditional libraries in four-year colleges and universities. This factor was perhaps in part because of the lower reading level of the students which increased the importance of utilization of non-print material in instruction. A comparison of the Association of College and Research Libraries' Guidelines for Two-Year College Learning Resources Programs (ALA, 1972) with various drafts of the four-year college standards underscored this difference in philosophy and activity.

Current trends in community colleges moved toward the combining of library and media (audiovisual) services into a single operation known by any of several titles: Library and Learning Resources Center, the Instructional Media Center, or the Educational Development Center. Usually this center included the production of materials, as well as the collecting and servicing of prepared content materials. These centers arose in response to the special requirements of community colleges; learners attending these colleges seemed to have special needs that required innovative and active response from learning resource personnel. These learners came with a wide range of backgrounds and abilities. Many of them read at or below tenth grade level and their speech and writing skills were also below conventional college level. The sheer numbers of students to be handled required the development of new techniques of instruction. A high proportion of community colleges were relatively new institutions. In terms of numbers of students served, it was not at all unusual for a community college to grow from zero to several thousand students in under five years.

Administrations are constantly seeking ways to increase the cost effectiveness of money spent for materials, personnel, space, and capital equipment, while simultaneously increasing the learning of students. Educational objectives should be arrived at by both faculty and students. Establishing priorities toward achieving these objectives and evaluating effectiveness of programs, both immediate and long range, presented complex problems. Research data, properly collected and evaluated would have aided; however, sophisticated evaluations of the activities of learning resource centers have been hindered by the pressures of the increasing number of students to be served.

Community college learning resource departments may perhaps have been reaching the beginning of this leveling off period in the 1970's, under the pressures of falling enrollment, the energy crisis, and the decline in federal support.

A review of the Analytic Reports and the Institutional Data sections of the series Library Statistics of Colleges and Universities issued by the Library Surveys Branch of the National Center for Educational Statistics of the U.S. Office of Education for 1961-62, 1963-64, 1967-68, 1968-69, and 1970-71, showed a remarkable growth during this decade of learning resources in public community colleges. The U.S. aggregate total number of volumes increased from 4,458,486 to 18,567,424; the aggregate operating budgets increased from $8,149,991 to $77,173,593. The mean number of volumes per institution increased from 13,592 to 23,276; however, the mean number of volumes per FTE student declined from 18.6 to 13.1. The mean operating expenditures increased from

$24,847 to $81,178, and the expenditure per FTE student increased from $24 to $55. A compilation of these increases in the size of collections, staff, and operating expenses for these years is shown in Table 2.

One of the most striking elements of these statistics was the extraordinary range between the median and the mean and the 90th or 75th percentile. This range became even more striking when the institutional statistics for 1971 were examined. Data on number of volumes, expenditure for print materials, audiovisual materials, salaries, and total operating expenses were key punched for all 638 two-year public colleges included in the Fall 1971 Institutional Data report. This report included some two-year technical institutes, some two-year semi-professional institutes, and some public junior colleges whose programs were exclusively liberal arts transfer, in addition to the comprehensive community colleges. Rank order listings were prepared for each of these characteristics, and decile divisions tabulated, as shown in Table 3. The lowest total operating budget was $8,682, and the smallest collection was 706 volumes; median operating budget was $81,328 and the median number of volumes was 22,828. Nevertheless, the range within the top decile was from $234,117 to $1,067,810 operating expenditures and from 49,159 volumes to 161,639 volumes. Some of the 64 libraries that placed high in total number of volumes were much further down the list in total operating expenses, and vice versa.

The study, then, sought to determine some of the reasons for this extraordinary range. Why were some college resource programs so much more expensive than others? Did they differ in kind, or just in size and degree from the median institutions? What was the relationship of total expenditure to age of the college and to enrollment? What

TABLE 2

VOLUMES, STAFF AND EXPENDITURES OF LIBRARIES IN PUBLIC TWO-YEAR COLLEGES
1961 - 1971

	1961-62			1963-64			1967-68		1968-69		1970-71	
U. S. Aggregate:												
Total Volumes	4,458,486			5,568,760			11,422,752		13,693,227		18,567,424	
Total Operating	$8,149,991			$12,433,183			$42,431,610		$50,926,600		$77,173,593	
	Averages			Averages								
	Median	Mean	90th %ile	Median	Mean	90th %ile	Mean	90th %ile	Mean	90th %ile	Mean	75th %ile
Volumes at end of year	10,173	13,592	28,013	11,000	14,889	30,448	21,883	41,924	23,732	44,093	23,276	34,752
Volumes per FTE student		18.6			16.6		12.		12.		13.1	
Total Personnel:	2.0	2.8	6.0	2.0	3.2	7.0	---	---	---	---	---	---
Professional	1.0	1.6	3.0	1.0	1.8	3.6	3.3	6.0	3.3	6.0	3.0	4.2
Non-professional	.5	1.1	3.5	1.5	2.3	4.6	3.4	8.0	3.7	8.0	2.6	5.0
Prof. per 1000 FTE students		.44			.49		2.39		.60		1.3	
Total Operating Expenditures	$ 14,698	24,847	52,863	21,886	33,243	39,153	81,287	167,866	68,261	184,455	81,178	137,862
Salaries & Wages	9,477	16,523	36,186	12,762	21,109	45,660	[54%]		[55%]		[60.8%]	
Materials & Binding	4,765	7,572	16,800	7,026	11,050	24,190	[40%]		[39%]		[31.8%]	
Other Expenditures	310	1,096	2,600	696	1,916	4,411	[5%]		[6%]		[7.3%]	
Expenditure per FTE student	$ 24	34	64	27	37	66	46		45		55	

Source: U.S.O.E. Library Surveys Branch. Library Statistics of Colleges and Universities

TABLE 3

DECILE CHARACTERISTICS OF 638 LIBRARIES IN PUBLIC TWO-YEAR COLLEGES IN 1971

Decile	Operating Budget	Salaries	Book Budget	AV Budget	# Volumes
Lowest	8,682	3,150	664	0	706
10	31,229	14,680	9,038	0	7,650
20	42,056	20,400	11,644	0	11,500
30	52,149	25,848	14,741	421	15,903
40	66,115	32,850	18,875	1,146	19,829
50	81,328	42,150	22,487	2,179	22,828
60	101,127	51,602	26,813	3,160	26,552
70	125,142	65,772	34,962	5,048	31,750
80	163,336	91,278	43,636	8,586	37,775
90	234,117	137,927	56,500	13,551	49,159
Highest	1,067,810	607,266	232,709	124,454	161,639

Source: Compiled by S. K. Thomson from USOE Library Surveys Branch Library Statistics of Colleges and Universities, Institutional Data, Fall 1971.

were the features of the various programs? What were the benefits to the user? Did the institutions differ markedly in per transaction cost? Could any type of cost benefit analysis be made from available institutional data on usage?

It was decided that the study would concentrate on visits to as many of the colleges in the top range of expenditures as time permitted. To ascertain which colleges to visit, a variety of approaches were considered. Since the key relationship being studied was user results vs. expenditures, it was important that a wide variety of programs be represented -- a wide range of poor to excellent, and a wide variety of age, enrollment, and size of learning resource staffs. It should be emphasized that the institutions visited were not selected because it was believed that their programs were excellent or outstanding, (although, of course, many were) but because their programs were relatively expensive. What were they getting for their money?

METHODOLOGY

The most comprehensive data available, the Library Statistics of College and Universities, Institutional Data, Fall 1971, was used to provide the sampling frame to determine which community colleges should be included in the survey. Among the known problems with using this data for the sample frame were: some multi-campus systems reported the whole system as one lump institution, others reported each campus; some new institutions, although they might have been recognized candidates for accreditation, and were offering instruction to several thousand students, were omitted; some colleges included both the library and all media services within their figures, others reported the library only;

a few major colleges were not reported; some colleges omitted production and instructional development from their reports. Therefore the comparison of per student cost from this data could be very misleading because of variance in reporting.

By the time the sample was being drawn, the Library Surveys Branch had received most of the 1973 HEGIS questionnaires. Since community colleges change so rapidly, this information was of great importance to the planning of this study. The study benefitted greatly from the extraordinary generosity and cooperation of the staff of the Library Services Branch in making available preliminary information for selected institutions from the 1973 HEGIS. They were also extremely helpful in discussing the problems and shortcomings of various measures of utilization of libraries.

The method of selecting the institutions to be included was to take the 1970-71 operating expenditures, the 1971-72 operating budgets, and the 1972-73 operating expenditures, and compute a mean expenditure for this three-year period. These means were ranked and the top forty colleges were arranged geographically, as shown in Figure 1.

These forty community colleges tended to be grouped around metropolitan areas, and were located in thirteen states:

Arizona 1	Michigan 1	
California 8	Missouri 1	
Florida 5	New Jersey 4	Texas 3
Illinois 3	New York 7	Virginia 1
Maryland 3	Ohio 1	Washington 2

After examining the map, the decision was made to visit community colleges in the Los Angeles, Dallas-Fort Worth, Saint Louis, Chicago, Cleveland,

FIGURE 1

LOCATION OF THE 40 COMMUNITY COLLEGES REPORTING THE HIGHEST EXPENDITURES FOR LEARNING RESOURCES 1970-73

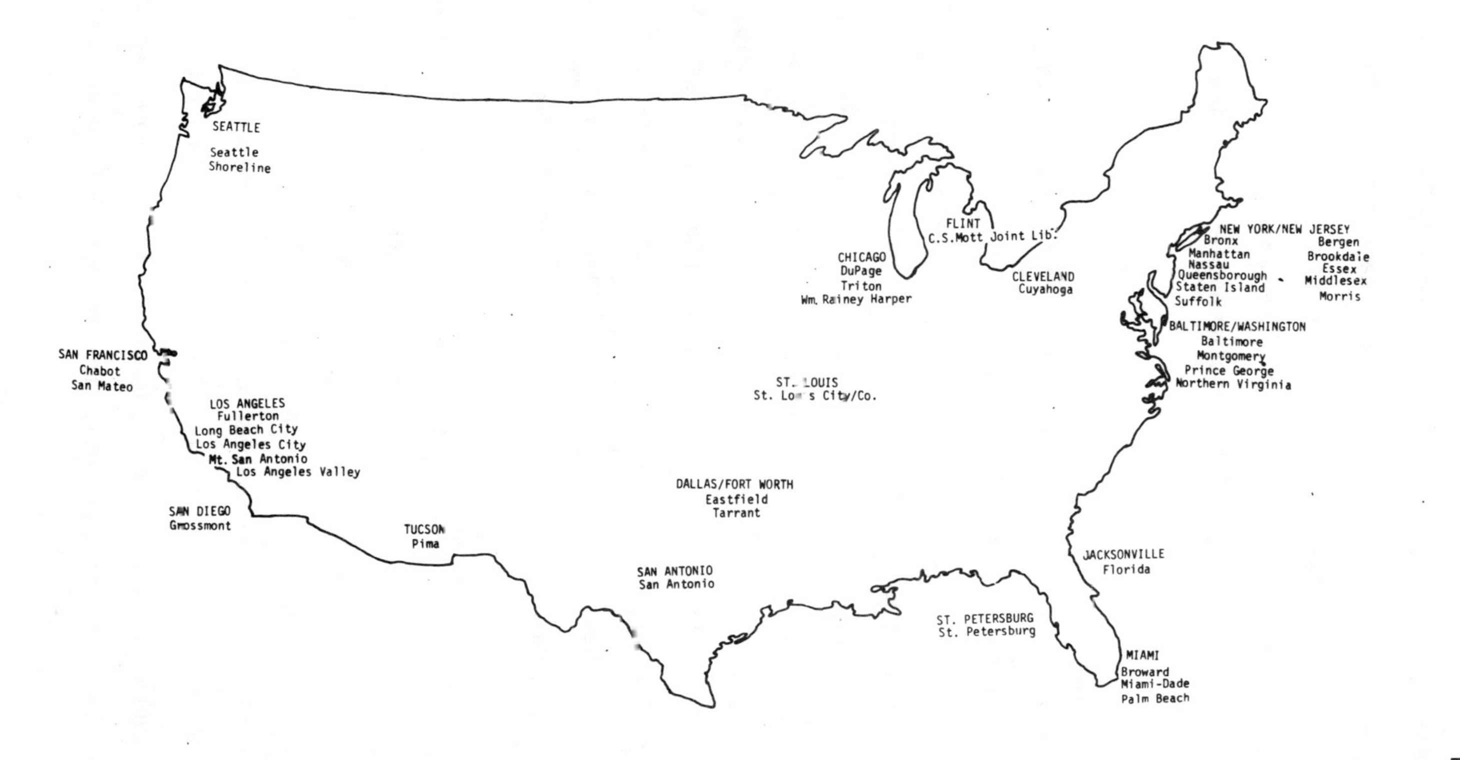

Miami, Baltimore-Washington, and New York-New Jersey areas. Twenty-seven campuses of twenty-one colleges or college systems, and three district offices were visited, usually spending one full day in each. A total of one hundred thirty-four people were interviewed. A list of the campuses visited and the individuals interviewed is included in Table 1.

Interview method

After sending an explanatory letter to the learning resource director or the library director of the twenty-seven colleges, a telephone call was made to discuss the project information to be gathered and to set up appointments. Each director was sent in advance a copy of the interview schedule and three data-gathering tables, on staffing, production, instruction and media advisement. In addition, the administrator was asked to have available the total and full-time enrollment for fall 1972 and 1973; the operating and capital expenditures for 1972-73; budgets for 1973-74; the 1973 HEGIS; statistics for 1972-73, or latest year available on circulation, use of audiovisual materials and equipment, attendance, and other measures of use, if available; and the staff organization chart.

The directors were asked to set up appointments for interviews with key personnel. Questions directed to the director and associate director began with, "Please describe briefly some of the outstanding features of your learning resource program." This question usually led to a fifteen-minute description of a wide range of activities which provided helpful clues and insights. Then the budgets, past and future trends, development, grants, purchasing, and utilization were discussed. Reference librarians and media utilization advisors were asked about accessibility, instruction and guidance in use, and selection of materials. Production staff were asked about budgets, facilities and equipment, kinds of production done, non-instructional production, and quality. Inquiries were made to the person suggested by the director about computer applications. Circulation heads and those responsible for classroom distribution of audiovisual materials and equipment were asked about their methods and problems. Periodicals heads were asked about methods of control acquisition and circulation. Since time was very limited, it was arbitrarily decided that technical services personnel would not be interviewed in most cases; however, central technical services in three large multi-campus districts were examined. A copy of the interview schedule was included in Appendix A. The three data-gathering tables (Appendix B, C, and D) sent to the directors on staffing, production, and instruction and media advisement were not successful; most directors thought that these analyses would be impossible because of overlapping responsibilities.

Before each campus visit, I reviewed the information available from directories such as American Junior Colleges, American Library Directory, and Biographical Directory of Librarians. Whenever possible, I arrived on campus at 7:00 a.m., had breakfast in the student cafeteria, I watched and listened to the students, looked around the student center, visited the campus bookstore and in this manner, I got a preliminary impression of the campus, the facilities and their condition. I also wandered around the library and the learning resource center as unobtrusively as possible to get my own impression before the interviews. Where possible, I looked through the college catalog (bulletin) and student newspapers.

Since money is a very sensitive area, care was taken to avoid anything which might threaten confidence. Not only did I avoid comparing any campus with any other, I did not discuss what I had been told by any staff member with any other staff member. In almost all cases, I was able to cover all the questions on the interview schedule.

Chapter 2

CHARACTERISTICS OF THE 27 CAMPUSES SURVEYED

The twenty-seven campuses and three district offices of twenty-one colleges selected to survey were all comprehensive community colleges, but they differed widely in age, size of student body, size of library collections, and operating budgets.

The oldest had been established in 1913, the most recent in 1973. They ranged in total enrollment from 3,022 to 27,648, the mean being 10,818, the median 9,625. Their FTE (full-time equivalent students) ranged from 1,533 to 13,547, the mean being 6,288 and the median 5,653. Table 4 shows the relationship between date founded and FTE enrollment. Seventeen of the campuses were within the 4,000-8,000 FTE students range.

Six of the campuses would probably be classed as inner city areas; the majority were suburban, many in relatively wealthy counties.

The book collections varied in size from 19,683 to 140,761. The median size was 53,000 and the mean was 60,895. Table 5 shows the relationship between date founded and size of book collection. Disregarding age, sixteen of the 27 campus book collections ranged between 40,000 and 80,000 volumes.

The number of books per FTE student ranged from 5.68 to 22.28, the mean was 9.77 and the median 8.74. This was significantly below the mean number of volumes reported for the national aggregate in the USOE reports for the decade 1961-1971, as shown in Table 2. No explanation was found for this unexpected finding. The lack of relationship between

TABLE 4

DATE FOUNDED AND FTE ENROLLMENT OF THE 27 CAMPUSES SURVEYED

FTE Enrollment	Date Founded					
	Before 1940	1946-1959	1960-1964	1965-1969	1970-1973	Row Totals
under 2000					2	2
2000 - 3999		1	1			2
4000 - 5999	1	1	4	5	1	12
6000 - 7999		1	1	2		4
8000 - 9999				2		2
10,000 - 11,999	2		1	1		4
12,000 - 13,999	1					1
Column Totals	4	3	7	10	3	27

TABLE 5

DATE CAMPUS LR WAS FOUNDED BY
SIZE OF BOOK COLLECTION

Volumes	Date Campus LR Was Founded					
	Before 1940	1946-1959	1960-1964	1965-1969	1970-1973	Row Totals
under 20,000					1	1
20 - 39,999				2	1	4
40 - 59,999		2	5	5		12
60 - 79,999	1		1	2		4
80 - 99,999	1	1		1		3
100 - 119,999	1		1			2
120 - 139,999						
140,000 and over	1					1
Column Totals	4	3	7	10	2	27

total size of the collection and number of books per FTE student was shown in Table 6.

The mean expenditure 1972-73 per FTE was $77.06; the median was $74.05, and the range $27.27 to $187.80. The total expenditures for 1972-73 ranged from $178,019 to $839,495 per campus. The mean was $434,659, the median was $395,724.

Of the twenty-seven campuses, five had learning resource centers which integrated into a single unit the personnel and resources responsible for print and non-print services. In twenty-two of the campuses, the library and the media services were operated as separate units, although in fourteen of these campuses, both were headed by a common administrator. This relationship was explained in greater detail in the chapter on staffing.

INFLUENCE OF OTHER CAMPUSES WITHIN THE ORGANIZATION OR DISTRICT

Many of the colleges visited were one unit of a multi-campus community college organization. The presence of other campuses competing for funds, and sometimes for administrative attention, occasionally had effects on the budget and organizational development of the separate units. In some districts a single dean of learning resources administered all units, with associate deans heading the campus LRC's. Other districts had a much looser coordination, perhaps a cooperation committee, or virtually no attempt at all at coordination and cooperation. Five of the campuses which had separate LRC administrations had relatively highly developed levels of voluntary cooperation, including shared materials and resources, combined instructional development workshops, often a daily shuttle bus for books and films, shared equipment and even

TABLE 6

NUMBER OF VOLUMES PER FTE STUDENT
BY TOTAL SIZE IN VOLUMES OF
BOOK COLLECTION

Volumes Per FTE Student	Size of Book Collection in Volumes								
	Under 20,000	20,000 39,999	40,000 59,999	60,000 79,999	80,000 99,999	100,000 119,999	120,000 139,999	140,000 and over	Row Totals
5		1	2						3
6			2						2
7		2	2	1	1	1			7
8		1	1						2
9			2		1				3
10			1			1			2
11				2					2
12 - 13	1							1	2
14 - 15			1	1	1				3
22			1						1
Column Totals	1	4	12	4	3	2		1	27

a shared warehouse. One college with voluntary cooperation between campus LRC's had a district coordinator of instructional development, who spent a day per week on each campus consulting with faculty and LRC staff.

Eight of the colleges had a very high degree of local autonomy. In some systems the policy was to put the money where the students were, but other campuses felt strongly that allocation bases solely on campus population could result in serious educational maladjustments. An inner city campus might have had much more need for special resources than an area where students were better prepared or better motivated. There were occasional situations where a strong initial campus with a relatively good collection had been built up with expectations of coasting on minimum funding while more current moneys were diverted to developing campuses. This might have done serious damage both to the currency of the collection, and also to the morale and user relations of the staff in the original campus. Often very serious inequities existed between the resources available to students at different campuses of the same college district. Some administrators felt that the current trend was toward widespread use of satellite teaching stations rather than toward development of additional fully appointed campuses. Others felt that development of these satellites were in truth very expensive and an uneconomical use of resources, since at best they could offer the students only limited resources. Multi-campus units often planned LRC facilities on each campus, but centrally retained certain common functions such as acquisition and cataloging, film rentals, production, equipment repair, and television.

The existing campus units often had a heavy responsibility toward the development of the new campus, often with no increase in help to select the materials, to acquire and catalog them, to plan the LRC space in the new buildings, to select furniture and equipment, and even to interview and select the staff.

Chapter 3

BUDGETS: ORGANIZATION, CATEGORIES, AND RANGES

Full 1973-74 budget listings were provided for analysis by twelve colleges representing 16 campuses and two district offices; in all cases all audiovisual and related production and engineering and library budgets were included. The remaining eleven campuses which provided only partial information were not included in the analyses in this section of the report.

These sixteen campuses represented a wide range cross section of the whole twenty-seven. Two large district systems, with their central production and technical processing units, were included. One of the five totally integrated learning resource centers was included; twelve of the campuses used separate library and audiovisual budgets; three others, although the library and the audiovisual service were separate units, did not show them as separate budgets.

The learning resources for these campuses were established at various dates from 1927 to 1973. The campuses ranged in size from 3022 to 27,648 total enrollment, (mean 12,104; median, 11,000), and in Full time equivalent students (FTE) ranged from 1,533 to 13,547, (mean 6,204; median, 5,500). The enrollments in FTE and the dates established are shown in Table 7. The ratio of FTE to total enrollment varied from 5:6 to 2:7; this relationship was shown in Table 8. This ratio is important for learning resource personnel and materials planning. The number of FTE determines the college income, and therefore the

TABLE 7

FTE ENROLLMENT VS. DATE THE LRC WAS FOUNDED
FOR 16 CAMPUSES WHOSE BUDGETS WERE
ANALYZED IN DETAIL

FTE	Date Founded					
	Prior to 1940	1945 1959	1960 1964	1965 1969	1970 1973	Row Totals
under 2,000					2	2
2,000 - 3,499			1			1
4,000 - 5,999	1	1	1	2	2	7
6,000 - 7,999		1		1		2
8,000 - 9,999				1		1
10,000 - 11,999			1	1		2
over 12,000	1					1
Column Totals	2	2	3	5	4	16

TABLE 8

ENROLLMENT AND FTE OF 16 CAMPUSES WHOSE BUDGETS WERE ANALYZED IN DETAIL

FTE	Total Enrollment					
	under 5,000	5,000 9,999	10,000 14,999	15,000 19,999	20,000 and over	Row Totals
under 5,000	2	3				5
5,000 - 9,999		2	4	2		8
10,000 - 14,999				1	2	3
Column Totals	2	5	4	3	2	16

proportionate income that can be expended for learning resources; but the learning resource staff must deal with the total number of warm bodies: there are that many individuals who must be taught how to use the card catalog, where materials are, how to use equipment, and even basic study skills and reading, writing and speaking. The higher the proportion of part-time students, the thinner the resource staff and materials must be spread; there is even greater need for multiple copies of materials and more need for circulating audiovisual equipment, since many of these students are on campus only once or twice a week and want to be able to take resources home for study purposes. The sixteen campuses had a combined total of 193,662 students, and a combined FTE of 99,265. They are located in eight states.

These sixteen campuses had total budgets, capital and operating, for learning resources ranging from $285,489 to $1,352,738, the mean being $519,829 and the median being approximately $450,000. The expenditure per FTE ranged from $27.31 to $226.12, the mean being $83.73 and the median being $96. In general, the expenditure per FTE tended to decrease as enrollment increased; the relationship between FTE enrollment and expenditure for learning resources per FTE was shown in Table 9. The relationship between the total dollar amount of learning resource budget and the expenditure per FTE was much more scattered, as shown in Table 10. As was expected, there was also a positive correlation between age of the learning resource center and expenditure per FTE, since both characteristics were related to enrollment. This relationship is shown in Table 11.

The budgets usually were organized first by administrative unit within the Learning Resource Center, such as Audiovisual, Library,

TABLE 9

FTE ENROLLMENT BY EXPENDITURE PER FTE

Expenditure per FTE Student	Under 2,000	2,000 3,999	4,000 5,999	6,000 7,999	8,000 9,999	10,000 11,999	over 12,000	Row Totals
25 - 49						1	1	2
50 - 74			2					2
75 - 99			3	1				4
100 - 124			2	1		1		4
125 - 149					1			1
150 - 174								
175 - 199	2							2
200 - 224								
225 & over		1						1
Column Totals	2	1	7	2	1	2	1	16

TABLE 10

TOTAL CAMPUS LEARNING RESOURCES BUDGET
BY EXPENDITURE PER FTE

Expenditure Per FTE	Total Campus Learning Resources Budget				
	250,000-499,999	500,000-749,999	750,000-999,000	1,000,000 and over	Row Total
25 to 49	2				2
50 to 74	2				2
75 to 99	2	2			4
100 to 124		3		1	4
125 to 149				1	1
150 to 174					
175 to 199	2				2
200 to 224					
225 and over	1				1
Column Totals	9	5		2	16

TABLE 11

DATE LEARNING RESOURCES FOUNDED
BY EXPENDITURE PER FTE

Expenditure Per FTE	Date Founded					
	Prior to 1940	1945-1959	1960-1964	1965-1969	1970-1973	Row Total
$ 25 - 49	1			1		2
50 - 74	1	1				2
75 - 99			1	1	2	4
100 - 124		1	1	1		3
125 - 149				2		2
150 - 174						
175 - 199					2	2
200 - 224			1			1
225 and over						
Column Total	2	2	3	5	4	16

Processing, Production, Engineering, etc. Within each of these units there were subdivisions by various categories of personnel, then general operating expenses, then capital, which in some cases included books. The following analyses were made following the categories actually designated within the budget documents with minor combining of synonym categories.

The aggregate total of all budgets for the sixteen campuses was $8,311,829. Of this, 69% was allocated for personnel, including full and part-time regular staff, student aids, work study, and fringe benefits. General operating, including books and materials, represented 24%. Capital, as here defined, including furniture and equipment, but excluding books and materials (regardless of whether they were considered capital items on some campuses) represented 7% of these sixteen budgets.

OPERATING BUDGETS

Personnel Budgets

The total personnel budget (for professional, semi-professional or technical assistants, and clerical or supportive staff, but excluding student assistance, work study and fringe benefits) ranged in the sixteen campuses from $70,826 to $478,289, the mean being $339,668, the median $237,380. The expenditure per FTE ranged from $17.03 to $124.76, the mean being $54.74 and the median being $47.82. This portion of the personnel budget represented from 50% to 93% of the campus budget for learning resources, the mean being 65% and the median 63%. Table 12 shows that there was a tendency for personnel expenditure per FTE to decrease as enrollment increased.

Professional personnel costs in the sixteen campuses was a mean

TABLE 12

FULL AND PART-TIME PERSONNEL EXPENDITURE PER FTE BY FTE ENROLLMENT

Full and Part Time Personnel Expenditure Per FTE	FTE Enrollment							
	Under 2000	2000-3999	4000-5999	6000-7999	8000-9999	10,000-11,999	Over 12,000	Row Totals
Under 25						1	1	2
25 - 49			4		1	1		6
50 - 74	1		2	1				4
75 - 99			1	1				2
100 - 124	1	1						2
Column Totals	2	1	7	2	1	2	1	16

of $190,112, median $153,482, and per FTE mean $30.64, median $26. Of the twelve campuses which divided their personnel budgets between library-related, and audiovisual-related units, the mean for the library units was $130,785 for professional personnel, and $58,770 for professional audiovisual personnel. A discussion of the organization of personnel will be found in a later chapter.

Nine of the campus learning resource budgets were charged for student aid. The mean was $16,441, the median $16,320. Three campuses were charged with work study wages; the amounts were $18,380, $8,960, and $7,000.

Six of the campuses were charged in the learning resource budgets for various employee benefits: Employee tuition waivers $165; Educational (staff) development $2,064; Fringe benefits, group insurance, tuition reimbursement, professional expense $18,440; and one three-campus district had an aggregate charge of $122,291 to learning resources for staff benefits.

Operating Expenses

The portion of the budgets for operating expenses, other than personnel, included books, periodicals, and other print materials, content audiovisual materials, including film purchase and film rental, supplies, which might be characterized by categories for office supplies, data processing supplies, instructional or audiovisual supplies, book processing, book catalogs, binding, printing and forms, data processing, guest lecturers and honoraria, advertising, professional fees, postage, telephone, freight, transporting of things, travel, equipment rental, copier expense, maintenance agreements and repairs, equipment replacement parts, and repair tools, and miscellaneous. For this analysis, books were always considered operating expense items, although they were sometimes considered a capital item by some campuses, particularly if the campus was new, and might be reimbursed by the state at a higher percentage than other operating expenses.

Books. The book budget, which included the periodical budget in at least four instances, ranged from $11,200 to $94,200 with a mean of $54,456 and a median of $50,000. This represents a per FTE student expenditure ranging from $3.86 to $41.37, with a mean of $8.67 and a median of $8.35.

The relationship between expenditure for books per FTE and the size of the book collection varied, as shown in Table 13. While expenditure per FTE for collections under 30,000 volumes was usually high, expenditures for collections greater than 40,000 did not diminish as the collection gets larger, as one might perhaps expect; on the contrary, it tended to rise. This might have indicated that administrators were becoming aware of the decay rate of information, and the necessity of continual addition to current material in a collection if it were to continue to serve the faculty and students.

Periodicals. Twelve campus budgets included separate budgets for periodicals, which sometimes specified that it included newspapers and microfilm; one campus had a separate budget for microfilm. These budgets ranged from $5,000 to $58,000 with a mean of $15,528 and a median of $12,300. Campuses varied as to whether they considered such expensive serials as indexes and abstracts as periodicals or books.

Total Print items. On the sixteen campuses, the combined budget for print items, including books, periodicals, etc., represented a mean of $66,099 and a median of $56,250. The per FTE expenditure was

TABLE 13

SIZE OF BOOK COLLECTION
BY EXPENDITURES FOR
BOOKS FOR FTE STUDENTS

Expenditures For Books Per FTE Student	Size of Book Collection in Thousands						
	Under 20,000	20,000 39,999	40,000 59,999	60,000 79,999	80,000 99,999	100,000 and over	Row Totals
$3.00 - 4.99			1			1	2
5.00 - 6.99			3		1		4
7.00 - 8.99			2	2			4
9.00 -10.99				1			2
11.00 -12.99					1	1	2
//////////////	//////////////	//////////////	//////////////	//////////////	//////////////	//////////////	//////////////
30.00 -45.00		1					2
Column Totals	1	2	5	3	2	2	16

a mean of $10.65, and a median of $10.51.

<u>Audiovisual content materials (software)</u>. Audiovisual materials purchased with content, such as 16 mm and 8 mm films, film loops, slides, overhead transparencies, tapes, cassettes, videotapes, etc. were specifically budgeted for in eleven of the campus learning resource budgets. Of the total sum almost half was specifically allocated to films; presumably the total amount spent for films was even greater, since some of the campuses which had film libraries included a lump sum not designated by type of AV material. The combined budgets for AV materials and films had a mean of $26,810. The median figure exclusive of district collections was $22,000.

<u>Instructional or audiovisual supplies</u>. All campuses and both district offices budgeted for instructional or audiovisual supplies (rawstock) including blank film, blank tape, videotape, acetates, etc. These budgets showed a mean of $18,798, and a median, exclusive of district offices, of $13,900.

<u>Film rental</u>. Ten learning resource budgets included a category for film rental; these ranged from $900 to $27,817 per campus, the mean being $10,214, the median $8,125.

<u>Aggregate audiovisual material expenditures purchased with content, rental, and rawstock)</u>. If one combined the audiovisual content materials, film, instructional or audiovisual supplies (rawstock), and film rental budgets on each campus, the mean expenditure was $42,765, and the median, exclusive of district offices, was $40,126. The FTE expenditure for these combined categories was a mean of $6.89, a median of $6.37 and a range of $1.24 to $31.11.

<u>Aggregate of purchased content materials</u>. If one combined the

book, periodical and newspaper, microfilm, audiovisual software, and film purchase budgets, the mean per campus expenditure was $84,722, and the median, exclusive of district offices, was $72,800. The FTE expenditure for these combined categories had a mean of $13.65 and a median of $12.74.

Print vs. non-print FTE expenditures. In general on these sixteen campuses, there was a positive correlation between the expenditure per FTE for print materials (books, periodicals, microfilm) and the expenditure per FTE for non-print materials (AV software, films, film rentals, and audiovisual supplies) -- one tended to rise as the other rose. Nevertheless, expenditures for print materials were greater than expenditures for non-print materials in all but two of the campuses. This relationship is shown in Table 14.

Other supplies. In addition to instructional or audiovisual supplies, every campus budget had one or more categories for other supplies; these categories were: office supplies, library supplies, data processing supplies, other supplies. The central tendency for the sixteen campuses in these aggregate categories (but not including instructional or audiovisual supplies) showed a mean of $10,184 and a median of $10,800. The range was $1,750 to $31,748.

Book processing. Three of the budgets showed amounts for book processing: $2675, $4500, and $32,700. The latter figure was included in the book budgets in the tabulation above, since the money included both the price of the books as well as the book processing.

Book catalogs. Two budgets included items for book catalogs: $1200 and $10,111.

Binding. Three budgets included a category for binding:

TABLE 14

PRINT (Books, Periodicals, Microforms)
VS. NON PRINT (AV Software, Films, Film Rental, and AV Supplies)
EXPENDITURE PER FTE
FOR 12 SYSTEMS REPRESENTING 16 CAMPUSES

FTE Expenditure for Print	FTE Expenditure for Non Print						
	$1 to 3.99	$4 to 6.99	$7 to 9.99	$10 to 12.99	$13 to 15.99	$16 and over	Row Totals
$1 - 3.99							
4 - 6.99	2		1				3
7 - 9.99	1		1				2
10 - 12.99		2	1	2		1	6
13 - 15.99							
16 and over				1			1
Column Totals	3	2	3	3		1	12

$4400, $3675, and $3000.

Equipment rental. A wide variety of equipment was rented by the learning resource sections, including data processing equipment, photocopiers, charging machines, theft detection devices, microforms equipment, production equipment, etc. Nine campuses had budget categories for equipment rental. The mean was $6,854, the median $4,200 and the range $1,247 to $18,558 per year. In addition, two campuses had categories specifically indicated as copier expenses: $1550 and $2205.

Maintenance agreements and repairs. Fourteen of the campuses included categories for maintenance contracts and agreements and/or repairs. The range was $700 to $6,232, the median $2350 and the mean $3422.

Equipment replacement parts. In addition to the maintenance and repair budgets above, two campuses had separate categories for equipment replacement parts: $5000 and $2502. Besides these, one three-campus district had a parts budget aggregating $54,035.

Tools. Two campuses had tool budgets, of $1300 and $1184.

Printing and forms. Eight campuses included a category for printing, which sometimes included forms. The amounts budgeted ranged from $370 to $10,365, the mean being $4,423.

Professional fees. One campus had an item of $20,500 for professional fees.

Data processing. In addition to data processing supplies, included with other supplies above, one campus included a $6,710 item for data processing.

Postage. Charges for postage were included in a few budgets:

$1500, $3056, and $2050 for a district.

Telephone. Three institutions representing five campuses included telephone charges: $6050 and $410 for single campuses and $8550 for a three-campus district.

Freight and transportation of things. Freight charges for one campus were $150, and for a three-campus district $1000. "Transportation of things" was budgeted at $2400 at the other three-campus district.

Travel. Fourteen of the campuses included travel expenses in their budgets. Most learning resource administrators felt very strongly the importance of their personnel being able to attend conferences regularly in order to keep up with this rapidly changing field. Almost no one felt their travel budget was as much as it should be. The range was $450 to $10,000, the mean $2,946.

Miscellaneous categories. One campus had a guest lecturer budget ot $500. One had an advertising budget of $735. Two had miscellaneous budgets of $100 and $1000.

Other operating expenses. Four campuses had lump sum budgets for other operating expenses, unspecified: $1,993; $2,740; $21,378; and $25,559.

CAPITAL BUDGETS

Capital budgets, in addition to the book items mentioned above, were included for fifteen of the campuses; the sixteenth had been "frozen out this year." The capital budgets usually included all four, or some combination of: instructional or audiovisual equipment; office equipment, instructional furniture, and office furniture. By far the largest of these categories was instructional or audiovisual equipment, accounting for over 90% of the total. The aggregate total of these categories for the fifteen campuses was $560,382. The mean was $37,359. In the two three-campus districts, approximately two-fifths of the total campus capital budget was allocated to district offices. Of the individual campuses, excluding district offices, the median was $19,585. The capital budget expenditure per FTE student showed a mean of $5.96, with a range of $0.73 to $35.79. Obviously, the capital budget for learning resources may vary widely from year to year within a given campus depending on the timing of construction or installation of a major facility, such as a learning lab or a television studio.

Chapter 4

BUDGET DEVELOPMENT, TRENDS, AND EXPENDITURE CONTROLS

Although historical precedent, the amount of money that had been spent on that category in the past, was the single largest factor determining future budgets, a variety of patterns of development, and methods of controlling the expenditure of funds after appropriation became apparent.

PROGRAM PLANNING AND BUDGETING SYSTEMS (PPBS)

Attempts at implementing Program Planning and Budgeting Systems (PPBS) had been sporadically undertaken on some campuses. These involved various degrees of efforts to (1) critically define broad goals and objectives; (2) lay out the structure of the program and show the organization of personnel by function; (3) set out the objectives for each program, and ways to measure effectiveness of the methods being used to accomplish the objectives; (4) detail every possible way of attaining each objective; (5) make a cost-effectiveness study of each alternative approach to each objective; and (6) establish criteria, rules, and standards by which to rank the alternatives in order of desirability.

One of the states visited had mandated PPBS, and the colleges visited within that state were developing their budgeting systems toward this system. One of the colleges was to be a pilot college in the study of the implementation of PPBS. Another multicampus district within that state had developed guidelines for its campus officers.

In two other institutions program budgeting was extensively used for justification of special or innovative programs, especially those involving installations, purchase of equipment, new personnel, and usually extensive production of materials. These programs were carefully evaluated in terms of numbers of students to be served, specific educational objectives to be met, effectiveness of instruction, expected life span of the materials created, personnel cost, maintenance cost, and therefore, cost-effectiveness in terms of expected FTE credit hours generated by the programs.

One college was fully utilizing a variant of PPBS called Program Analysis, Objectives and Goals. Each department and administrative unit presented its needs in the budget document in terms of:

1. Program Analysis--the responsibilities of the unit
2. Progress in FY 1973, expressed in specific terms
3. Program Progress and Plans for FY 1974
4. Program Objectives for Budget Year 1975
5. Long range goals (FY 1976-1980)

One advantage of program budgeting for a complex operation includes the avoidance of the risk of imbalance in funding among components.

Learning Resource Centers need support in at least five areas in order to function:

1. Personnel
2. Facilities and Equipment
3. Prepared materials (published print and non-print materials, purchased with content)
4. Raw stock and processing for production
5. Maintenance and related overhead

When budgets are developed by simple categories of expenditures, trustees or governmental funding bodies make cuts which create an imbalance between these components which seriously hampers the program. Some of the most common imbalances are these: (1) disproportion between professional and clerical staff, resulting in inefficiencies; (2) very expensive installations without sufficient staff to operate them enough to justify their cost; (3) inadequate staff for sufficient liaison work with the faculty to permit meaningful integration of the Learning Resource program into class instruction; (4) reinventing the wheel by reproducing programs which have already been made many times instead of purchasing, elsewhere, cooperating, and modifying; (5) perpetuation of organizational units which no longer operate at maximum efficiency or educational effectiveness; and (6) inadequate maintenance to keep the facility operating efficiently.

MANAGEMENT BY OBJECTIVES

The administrative practice of Management by Objectives involves a joint definition of goals by management and by staff, the outlining of each staff member's responsibility toward those goals and methods of measuring his performance of those responsibilities, and using those measures to guide the operation of the unit, and evaluate the staff.

Management by Objectives was operational to a sophisticated and highly developed degree in eight of the colleges visited. These eight colleges divided into several patterns: Five had highly integrated programs of print and non-print services; two had library and media programs which were housed in the same building and had a common dean, but which were essentially separately run programs; and one college had library and media programs entirely separated in administration and location. These management objectives influenced the budget not only in the establishment of priorities, but also in the development of long range planning, five year programs, and in day-to-day operation.

MBO-oriented LRC's had spent considerable effort and time in the development of statements of objectives that are specific, measurable, limited in time, and realistic. They had systematic and regular assessments of their progress toward their objectives, and evaluations of personnel performance, based on performance criteria with individual responsibility outlined. Since the staff worked with the administration in this form of participatory management, motivation for achievement was high, and direct supervisory responsibility reduced. Decision making authority was spelled out at each level. Mini systems analyses were ongoing; operational models of processes and responsibilities were spelled out. Progress toward objectives was documented in a variety of specific ways, and evaluation data was systematically collected.

This often resulted in sharper codification of responsibilities--especially managerial authority at the lower middle management level, with development of manuals of policies and procedures. Since staff were involved in this codification process, accountability was more realistic.

In at least two of the eight institutions, MBO was closely tied into a heavy institutional commitment to the systems approach of instruction, with special attention to documentation of student educational achievement and the cost effectiveness of instructional techniques.

PAST TRENDS AND CURRENT SITUATION

Each administrator was asked to summarize the budget trends at his institution for learning resources. Institutional budgets for learning resources varied widely as a percentage of the institutional educational budget. It was very difficult to get good comparative figures, because some colleges included both the library and audiovisual services in a common figure; in others the same services may have been split among four or five departmental budgets.

To some extent the budget was related to the placement of each institution along the developmental scale. Some of the institutions visited were still young enough to be purchasing the initial collection and initial equipment. Others have achieved various stages of maturity; therefore, their expenditures for materials and equipment were leveling off or being reduced.

Budgets often, but not always, reflected the impact of enrollment upon the college. Four of the colleges reported steady increases of approximately 10% per year in the budget for learning resources. Occasionally, increases as high as 20% per year were reported. Some of these schools felt that the trend would slow up somewhat but continue to increase at at least 6%. One learning resources budget had doubled in the last four years, and was projecting doubling again in the next four. It should be remembered that the colleges selected were chosen because over the last three years they had reported spending at least $300,000 on learning resources (per college, not necessarily per campus).

Eleven other colleges reported that they were doing very well in the budget race. They spoke of feeling that administrations were very good to them, of having the absolute conviction and support of the administration, and of getting real encouragement to the faculty in the use of media and learning resources. They spoke of being able to go to the President when they had a real need; they would present their case and have the request approved down to the last wire. Several of these schools spoke of getting anything they wanted and of never having been refused anything. Those schools regarded spending as being largely up to the learning resources administrator. They spoke of their President's having said, "What's good for you is good for the college."

Administrators spoke of the importance of healthy relationships with the college administration and of having administrators understand the needs of libraries and learning resources. The attitude of the LRC administrator in the preparation and presentation of the budget was important. Several attitude guidelines were stressed: a) The need to present the programs fairly and clearly in terms of their educational effect b) Importance of tact and humor, and the desirability of being low-key, but not a yes man.

On the other hand, nine of the colleges felt that at best they were just "holding their own" in the budget trend. In many cases their budgets were very conservative; although the dollar amount had perhaps been increased, the purchasing power had stayed the same or declined somewhat. This was to a large extent related to the enrollment picture. Several of the colleges visited had been very hard hit by failures of enrollments to meet growth predictions, and some of them had experienced very severe budget cuts as a result. In some cases these cuts had been as early as 1970, and now they felt that the trend was once again upward. In one case, although the enrollment was above prediction this year, it was not possible to restore the budget cuts, because the personnel contracts absorbed the increase. One administrator felt that in the early years, his department had routinely overspent, and that the cuts were bringing things back into a more appropriate and realistic appraisal of needs.

In eight of the colleges there was a definite downward trend in their budgets. Those colleges had to fight for whatever they got; they felt that they had to rob Peter to pay Paul, and that they were unable to develop services or grow as they had planned. Facilities delays were common almost everywhere, and developments had had to be postponed or cancelled in many places. At the time of the campus visits, it was not yet known what effect the gas shortage would have on the spring enrollments.

Stress varied on the amount and kind of documentation presented in support of the budget. Some administrators felt that it was wasted paper that no one ever read, others felt that it was a very healthy exercise beneficial on both sides: in forcing the LRC staff to clarify its thinking and weigh its priorities, and helpful in increasing the understanding of the college administrators for the Learning Resources program.

One of the frequently hit areas in these budget cuts was the book budget. Declines from 6C to 75% in these funds were reported, not even allowing for increased inflation eroding the actual purchasing power.

Occasionally an administrator would indicate that one aspect or area of the program had been a stepchild with inadequate budget or space or personnel at the expense of another. Some administrators felt that to have reached a plateau of growth was perhaps a desirable thing, that this would consolidate the programs and services now offered.

FUTURE

While many of the administrators felt that it was impossible to tell where the budgets would probably go in the future, about a third were relatively optimistic. Some anticipated rapid increases in funding. They felt they were more than pulling their weight, that the programs which were needed would be expanded further. Others felt that things would get worse. Some felt that they had not really been hurting in the past, but they sensed that there would be more and more competition for institutional funding. A few felt they would be lucky not to slide backward; that the best they could hope for was to maintain present levels. One spoke of automation as requiring substantial increases in funding over manual systems. Some boards were moving toward formula increases or proportions, which were often not up to inflation rates. Such programs as individualized instruction and course offerings by cable television were seen to require substantial increases in learning resource money. There was frequent reference to a trend to supporting more spectacular aspects of the Learning Resource programs but a reluctance to spend money maintaining more conventional resources; this was regarded as a leaning to the new, the innovative, the news-making.

CUTS, FREEZES, BONUSES

Independent of the budget trends from year to year, a number of institutions have experienced cuts or freezes within the budget year; often because enrollment, and therefore income, did not meet projections. Occasionally, learning resource departments have had unexpected increases in allocations of funds when enrollments significantly exceeded expectations.

Eight of the colleges had never had any cut or freeze problem. They made statements such as, "Admirable administration: Very above board, open and honest." "We always spend our budget; we're proud of being able to spend it." One college attributed not having cuts or freezes within the last three years to improved budgeting processes and fiscal management.

Five other colleges had regular and systematic fall reviews of the fiscal situation--the actual vs. the planned income--which adjusted the budgets up or down accordingly. One college regularly put holds on new positions until the enrollment was final. Sometimes the increase in budgets because of over-enrollment, for both personnel and materials, had been substantial. Thirteen of the colleges had experienced cuts and freezes when enrollments were low, without increases when enrollments exceeded predictions. Often the cuts took the form of unusually early and abrupt spring cut-offs of funds; therefore, some of the learning resource centers were following the practice of spending all of each year's equipment budget, and purchasing many types of supplies and materials immediately at the start of each fiscal year. This practice, of course, left them with no money for any new needs that might arise during the fiscal year. Some LRC's were able to continue to buy when budgets were cut completely in certain areas by maneuvering out of other funds. Occasionally budgets were frozen by state legislatures or other governmental administrative units without any relationship to the enrollment or the local college situation. During freezes, personnel was often the hardest hit budget line: leaves were not filled, open positions were frozen or done away with, part-time or non-tenured positions were released, and occasionally even tenured faculty had to leave. Some LRC's had a May, or even March cut-off; if they did not spend by that date, they would lose a corresponding amount from the next year's budget as well.

Occasionally an administrator took the attitude that the cuts were not serious because he considered that they represented a delay or postponement in development, rather than final curtailment of the activity.

Some colleges were quite actively seeking ways to reduce the contributing problems of low enrollment, especially gas shortages. Among the solutions being proposed was the establishment of many more store-front satellite teaching areas to take more of the classes to the students. Of course, this presented obvious problems for learning resource departments, particularly in the availability to all of the book collection.

Strategies for combatting cuts were often forceful; "If people get cut, the only way to get them back is not to do stuff until people holler and you get the staff back. If you establish priorities and do the things they want most, the rest will pile up until you never get out from under."

BUDGET DEVELOPMENT

At least three fundamentally different starting points have significant effects on how learning college budgets are developed:

1. Some colleges have a fixed tax rate for their support. This tax rate, combined with their enrollment projections, can enable them to predict their income; therefore, they can start with a total sum and divide it among the departments.

2. Some colleges are informed of the dollar amount allocated to each campus, and they decide locally how to split it up.

3. Some colleges request funds of a governing body, and the sum allocated is not fixed by law or by formula. Therefore, each department submits a blue sky draft which is cut by a succession of deans, boards and committees up the line--without regard, necessarily, for the balance of programs.

Historical precedent was by far the most significant factor in determining LRC budget for most of the colleges. What was spent or allocated in prior years was adjusted in some cases, for changing circumstances; or perhaps, it was inflated by a predetermined percentage formula.

Staff Input

A few of the learning resource administrators said they developed the budgets themselves with little or no input from their staffs, perhaps because the budget had to be developed so far in advance. Most administrators, however, relied significantly on input from key members of their staff. Staff were asked what they wanted, and what they wanted to develop. Members of the staff developed estimates and priorities, realistic projections of needs, and sometimes detailed surveys of adequacy by department or subject area. This type of participatory management, most administrators felt, repaid the effort it took in staff morale: "It's a good place for letting people do their jobs; excellent relationships result when each feels he is not only asked, but heard, and his needs met."

Sometimes, when the learning resource center had decided to allocate the materials budget by department, the LRC staff had primary responsibility for dividing that budget; sometimes this responsibility was shared with the department chairman, or with a faculty committee.

Sometimes the administrator shared with the staff not only responsibility for input on the development of the budget, but even for its defense. "My troops and I show up in force at all Board of Trustee meetings where they are considering anything at all controversial for us; we have built up a good working relationship with the Board by clearly presenting rationale, and by always doing our homework. We don't leave it up to the Deans or President to present our case." Some of the written justifications developed by the staff covered each code page by page; some merely justified unusual items.

Faculty Input

Less than half of the learning resource administrators regularly and systematically received input from the faculty in the development of the LRC budgets. However, those who worked toward this aspect felt the results very beneficial, especially in faculty backing for their programs. Many presidents were far more impressed by faculty requests for LRC services than by requests or proposals from the LRC itself. Many expected LRC budget justification to be based on faculty demand for service. "You show us that faculty will use, and we will fund to buy."

Input from the faculty came in a variety of ways. Some LRC's assigned a member of the LRC staff as a formal liaison with each faculty department; these LRC staff members met with the department, cooperated in selecting and weeding materials, and served as a budget request channel.

Some LRC's used the Faculty Learning Resources Committee as a channel for expressing faculty needs. Sometimes these committees had student members. Some of these committees were responsible not only as advisory groups; they also had some administrative responsibility in approving or rejecting specific requests and monitoring expenditures.

Most commonly, input was obtained by the head of the LRC from the chairmen of the academic departments or from the division heads. Each request was documented as far as possible--detailing who was going to use it and why. As far as possible, broad based consensus and commitment to use was obtained before major purchases are made. Each January, one LRC head sent each department chairman a form for indicating his needs for the forthcoming budget. Another chairman found it more effective to meet with each chairman, then writing up a statement for their approval, including what programs they hoped to develop, innovations they desired, services they would like, and materials they needed. This document served as a safeguard for the LRC as well as a planning document. This exchange increased the understanding of each for the other. The comment was made that "they look forward to these meetings, which are fruitful; they get what they want; and it is sound educationally." These documents were done in as much detail as possible; the more specific, the better it became for budget development.

Some LRC administrators held staff meetings of all professional staff to determine priorities and rankings of requests, and to further assist in justification. Consensus of the professional staff determined the priorities submitted.

DEVELOPMENT OF THE BUDGET BEYOND THE LRC

Campuses had various patterns of developing the consolidated budget from the various departmental requests submitted. In most campuses, the major decision making was done by a combination of upper level administrators; deans, president, and business administrators. Sometimes there were formal hearings at which the department chairmen could defend their programs; sometimes not. The degree to which the top administrators involved middle level administrators in the decision making process varied widely. Some Presidents made a deliberate effort to keep the communication and decision making as open as possible; some took a very authoritarian attitude. Some colleges left the budget negotiation to a free and open discussion between the deans, which became leadership value judgments--"All come together and pare down and resubmit, but everyone keeps everyone else honest, and the result is that everyone has a fair shake."

A few campuses had a strong faculty committee who had a real share in the decision making process. Usually this committee held local hearings about budgetary recommendations. Sometimes the chain of development of the budget was very long, and decision making became further and further removed from the people who had to carry out the responsibilities. The chain could include chairmen, deans, local campus presidents, district vice-presidents, district presidents, chancellors, provosts, local and district boards, local and district governing bodies, and even state boards and legislatures.

How far the head of the LRC was from the person who had the single most important amount of decision making power varied. Some administrators were directly in line with that person; some were as many as four steps removed. That individual was not always the president; sometimes, it was a vice-president or a dean or a business administrator, a chancellor or vice-chancellor. Often the learning resources administrator had two bosses: the campus dean of instruction or academic affairs, and the district vice-president for business administration, or some other combination. Some administrators noted a trend to decision making at a lower level, for more realistic adjustments, getting away from pyramid authority, toward more "equitable distribution of dissatisfaction."

FLEXIBILITY

Obviously, since budgets were usually made up a year in advance, and since community college Learning Resource Centers were dynamic organizations generally alert to the latest developments in methods, materials, and equipment, the degree of flexibility permitted in the actual expenditure of the budget, once appropriated, was of considerable importance to most administrators.

Both the degree of flexibility and the amount of autonomous authority in the decision making varied from institution to institution. In some colleges, once the line had been approved, the LRC administrator could spend the funds with no further approvals by deans, presidents, business administrators, etc., necessary. In other colleges, this approval was more or less pro forma. In still others, each expenditure was subjected to scrutiny de novo; and the justification process, already done for the budget defense, was redone.

Three main categories comprised most of the LRC budgets examined: capital, salaries and wages, and materials and operating expenses. Within these categories, there was usually at least some degree of flexibility, but transference between the categories was often severely restricted.

Ten of the administrators indicated that they had plenty of flexibility, ranging from total freedom and flexibility, to "enough"; and that approval, if required at all, was a very simple matter--just a routine notification.

In one college, transfers and shifts were a routine college-wide part of the mid-year and three-quarters budget review operation. Thirteen of the LRC administrators' transfers required formal approval by various higher officials: Boards of Trustees (2), college president (1), state department (1), vice-president (1), deans (2), business administrator (2), district officers (1), college administrative council or other administrative group (3). This approval, although "sometimes easy" was usually "hard to get" and "not done lightly."

In general, the most restricted budget category was capital. At least eight LRC's reported almost no flexibility within the capital and equipment funds. These were line item budgets and could be used only for the piece (or type) equipment specified in the budget.

The next most restricted budget category was personnel. This might be restricted between two or three categories of personnel, such as professional (faculty rank or certificated), semi-professional, and supportive staff (clerical). Sometimes the division was made further between full and part-time. For administrative purposes, these categories were important because fringe benefit costs to the college might vary widely between the groups; most of the colleges had quite specific staff contracts. Therefore, in general, maneuvering within the personnel category tended to require formal approval, if it was permitted at all. Sometimes, but not always, the stronger the staff negotiating units, the more inflexible the control.

Three of the LRC administrators reported no flexibility whatever. One of them was controlled by a state law not permitting transfers; another institution "treats our thirteen categories like thirteen locked boxes."

The situation could be further complicated by the degree of accountability for instructional department funds transferred into the LRC budget; in some colleges, this could be used at the discretion of the LRC director; in most it was a strict paper transfer used specifically for the content materials or raw stock for which the department had been charged. Some colleges permit the LRC to retain library fine money to use at its discretion.

ACCOUNTING METHOD (ACCRUAL OR CASH BASIS)

Since delivery of many types of library materials and equipment might take three months or more from the time of placing the order, the method of accounting for funds--whether cash basis or accrual--was influential in the administration of learning resources. If an institution was on a cash basis, and required a cut-off of orders in April or even earlier, some orders had to be cancelled after the library has already waited several months for the item; or there was a several month gap during which it could not order materials. This produced obvious unevenness in the flow of materials through the acquisitions and cataloging departments, and might have proved a serious inconvenience to the instructional faculty. Some administrators would argue that this cut-off was beneficial; they thought it forced staff and faculty to plan ahead, and not to rely on last minute rushes and impulses. Obviously, the method of accounting affected the business manager's cash flow, which might be very uneven, depending upon the tuition schedule and the arrangements with the supporting governmental agency.

Seven of the institutions reported being on a strictly cash basis: materials must have been received and the bills paid, or they would lose the money. Two others were on cash basis for everything except books. One was on cash basis except for bid and contracted items. Twelve were on accrual or encumbrance basis: funds were considered expended at the time the order was placed, whether or not it had been received; of these, four had to have received and paid for the item by the end of the next fiscal year (the item could not be carried forward more than one fiscal year).

ACCOUNTING AND BUDGET REPORTS OF EXPENDITURES

Fifteen of the colleges had supposedly regular reports of expenditures by budget category from a central accounting or purchasing department. These varied widely in the degree that the learning resource administration found them satisfactory and could rely on them. Two of these were scheduled weekly, one bi-weekly, and the rest monthly.

Seven administrators expressed satisfaction with the college account reports, finding them to be on time, accurate, up-to-date, and dependable and reliable. In one college the LRC administrator told about "an excellent person in the computer system who has a good working relationship with both the controller's office and the LRC," who issued weekly reports that were highly accurate, detailed and up-to-date. In addition to the weekly listing, further detailed analyses could be had on two-hour demand; and for certain key summaries, immediate information was available on display through CRT's. In one state, all accounting and bookkeeping was done by state contract with an outside accounting firm.

Six colleges were very dissatisfied with the college accounting reports and found that they had to keep their own, since the reports were from 2 weeks to 6 weeks behind, and often inaccurate. One college LRC reported that it had never received final year-to-date reports, and that it was very difficult to ascertain what it had finally been charged with by account. In two colleges the frustration level was high; after digging down in the college report and analyzing all the errors, they found it almost impossible to get central accounting to correct them. These errors tended not only to be reflected in the reports made to boards and governing bodies, but also to be influential on action on subsequent budgets.

NON-CHARGE ITEMS

College administrations, government bodies and even interested taxpayers frequently wanted comparative figures on per student costs from college to college, particularly between state-supported (or partially supported) colleges. The U.S. Office of Education's, Library Statistics of Colleges and Universities, Institutional Data (Part B, Fall 1971, Table 1) included operating expenditure figures for each library per FTE student and per FTE faculty member. These figures were not only meaningless, but very misleading if used on a comparative basis, as they often were, because of the extreme heterogeneity of the expenses included. For some colleges the library only was included; for others the statistics incorporated the full range of learning resources, including very sophisticated television and other production. These discrepancies arose because instructional development might or might not be a function of the earning esource department. Even comparing budgets of earning esource departments with similar programs could be somewhat misleading, because no two budgets were constructed in exactly the same way; various institutions had different policies for charging items.

One of the objectives of the study was to ascertain the possibility of devising a formula for cost inclusion which would give a common data base to all, and which would permit fair, reliable, valid and replicable comparisons. In addition to variance in programs included, a significant variation is caused by different ways of charging certain items; some institutions charge these items to the departmental budgets, others charge them to the institutional budget. The situation was further complicated by whether or not the LRC charged back to department budgets such items as materials, raw stock, and labor. Another complication arose from the question of whether or not the LRC, in turn, was charged back for services it used, such as computer services and data processing.

Each director was asked to list items for which his department wasn't charged and which it needed to operate. It should be recognized that this list, shown in Table 15, was probably neither all inclusive nor mutually exclusive. Obviously, such items as fringe benefits, computer services, data processing, AV materials and film rentals, student aid, and maintenance of equipment could be very substantial expenditures, and the inclusion or omission from the learning resource budget could make significant differences in reported per student cost.

TABLE 15

NUMBER OF COLLEGES CHARGING OR NOT CHARGING LEARNING RESOURCE DEPARTMENTS, BY CATEGORY

Budget Category	Charged	Not Charged
Binding	[most]	1
Computer supplies	1	
Computer produced microform catalogs		1
Computer service and data processing	5	15
CRT terminals, and other input/output devices	1	4
Book catalogs	1	2
Travel		3
AV materials/film rentals/software		4 [transfers from depts.]
Use of district or regional films		2
Cataloging and acquisition		2 campuses
Student aid	10	3
Student work/study (institutional share)	3	9
Teletype		1
District production of AV materials		2
Maintenance of equipment	13	3
Repair contracts	3	4
Maintenance of office equipment	3	5
Theft control systems	1	1
Secretarial and office supplies	10	4
Photocopy, duplicating	3	3
Small remodeling or alterations	5	3
Telephones	3	14
Postage	2	12
Driver for vehicle	1	
Vehicles, gas, and repair	2	7
Printing done on campus	5	2
Fringe benefits	4	4

PURCHASING AND BIDDING

Learning resource center directors have to cope not only with college purchasing and bidding policies, but often with city, county, district, and/or state regulations as well.

Many of the learning resource centers acted as their own purchasing agent for content items: books, periodicals, audiovisual materials, microforms, etc., and placed their own orders directly with vendors.

For three of the colleges, all orders larger than $50 had to be sent through the state purchasing office; even so, it was occasionally possible to push through orders in a few hours if need was urgent. In seven other colleges, the college purchasing office placed all orders including content material, but in three of these the LRC typed the orders. In these latter three cases, the sending of orders by the purchasing department was automatic, usually not delaying the order by more than a week, sometimes by as little as a day. Receiving and payment was also handled by two of these purchasing departments. Three of the districts visited had central district acquisition of content materials; two other colleges directed their orders through the city purchasing department.

Administrators emphasized the importance of good working relationships with the purchasing departments, of very active communication and constant effort each to understand the problems of the other. "We learn to play the game;" "We can live with their rules;" "We both try to work out what is most convenient and rational." Problems arose out of failure on either side to follow through as expected; some red tape could be very time consuming, both in personnel time and in lag in delivery. Relatively few LRC administrators felt this to be a real problem area; one reported turn around time from order to receipt to be about eighteen months.

Bidding requirements varied from "virtually non-existent" or "very lax" to "very strict, iron-clad." The restrictions might be imposed by the college board of trustees, the city, county, district, state, or some combination thereof. The requirements and stringency of regulations usually varied with the amount of the purchase: under a certain amount (range $200-$2,500) verbal quotes only were required; next category (range $300-$2,500) written quotes, sometimes a number, 3 or 4, were required; higher category ($1,500-$10,000 minimum range) required public advertising, usually with publically opened bids. In addition, Board of Trustees or Presidential approval was often required if over a certain amount (often $2,500). Some institutions used a vendor list (any vendor could ask to be included) to request bids instead of public advertising. Most of the colleges could use state or county contract items in place of public bid if they felt it was to their advantage; in three instances this use of state contracts was not optional, but mandatory.

In addition to the time consumed by the bidding process, some administrators felt that bidding worked to their disadvantage in a variety of ways: in one instance, the institution was required to select an in-county vendor if at all possible; service and delivery times as well as prices were affected, since the low bid would not always represent the lowest available price. In some cases, the director knew he could buy the item cheaper off the shelf at some other dealer. Salesmen were often reluctant to demonstrate or to let equipment be examined for potential maintenance problems if they knew they might not get the bid.

Other LRC's negotiate blanket contracts for supplying items like audiovisual raw stock, film, tape, supplies, library supplies, lamps, repair parts, and office supplies; these were placed on demand at a set price during a period of time. These blanket contracts usually represented like items. Problems arose, however, despite good prices, particularly if the vendor failed to keep all items in stock; in these instances, the LRC had to wait sometimes 2 to 6 weeks, sometimes longer, in spite of the contract. One college is very active in a local college consortium for blanket bulk purchasing of this kind.

Specifications for bids were usually the responsibility of the LRC, and regulations varied. Some LRC's were permitted to specify brand and model; in those cases, some required the vendor to bid on that brand and model, others permitted the vendor to bid an alternate. When an alternate was permitted, it was usually the responsibility of the LRC to show why the alternate was not acceptable, if that was the case. The difficulties of writing functional performance specifications for some items, particularly some kinds of raw stock, were often mentioned. Sometimes LRC's were required to write specifications that were entirely functional, not technical, and they were not permitted to use trade names or models. The amount of cooperation and understanding the LRC received from the purchasing department in rejecting alternatives varied, but they all were required to show why the alternative was not up to specifications. Often the specifications were very detailed; sometimes priority specifications were not allowed. Any vendor should be able to bid it if he could deem specification by function. In general, "lock out bids" were not permitted; however, special problems occurred when equipment had to be compatible with existing equipment. Occasionally, LRC's have had to get outside consultants to defend their specifications or evaluations of options.

Specifications for custom items or installations had to be very specific and detailed to make competitive bidding at all realistic. Purchasing departments differed in the degree to which they wanted, or were willing to permit LRC's to make initial contacts with vendors, to get estimates, or to get commercial help in writing specifications.

CAPITAL BUDGET

Although at least three of the LRC directors thought that their capital budget was very generous, and that they could buy virtually anything they wanted, two-thirds of the LRC directors felt they were really deficient in capital money. Often the capital budget was a line item budget, specifying each piece of equipment; and little, if any leeway was allowed in spending the money for some other type of equipment. Some of the equipment budgets were more general, and stated the area of use, or in general what it was to do, without quantities or types. Sometimes this justification included:

1. Usage within overall community college program
2. Number of students who would benefit
3. Educational goals to be met
4. Cost compared to comparable approaches
5. Anticipated yearly maintenance and upkeep
6. Funds for supplies
7. Supervisory time required

In nine colleges very substantial outlay for equipment was made as part of a new building; this was charged against the cost of the building, which was often bond money. Sometimes building money was funded by the state at a somewhat higher ratio than operating money. How adequate this initial equipment remained varied with the type of installation, its age, the growth rate of the institution, and changing technology. Sometimes, these buildings were initially shared as classrooms, and the LRC moved into them gradually, with varying degrees of adequacy in the renovation and equipment funding. In a few cases, building money had been available, but no equipment money; budget crunches had delayed a lot of plans. Some college administrators had planned to coast for far too long on the building money, and equipment had become obsolete and outworked.

Eight other colleges reported that they had had little or no capital money in the last few years for new equipment; that in the early days they had been able to keep abreast of technological improvements and innovations, but not any more. Some capital budgets were not even firmed up until the fiscal year was half over; they still were not able to buy some items that had been top priority for several years. This inability to keep up with the changing technology hurt not only the production capability, but even the ability to utilize new types of commercially available materials in new formats. In some schools, the replacement problem was particularly acute; some major equipment was seven to ten years old, and worn out or obsolete, with repair parts no longer available. Some schools did have a regular budget item for replacing equipment, and two schools had a sinking fund for future needs. A few of the colleges were routinely planning to replace most equipment on a five year cycle. Some schools were feeling the need so badly that they had swapped operating expense money for equipment.

Some administrations were willing to spend for big, showy production configurations, but not for the every-day workhorse kinds. Some colleges allocated the equipment budget to departments and divisions; how much control the LRC had over the selection, operation, maintenance, and use under those conditions varied.

SPACE ALTERATION AND REMODELING

Although many of the colleges visited had relatively new buildings, about a fourth were badly in need of space, and were trying to serve several times as many students as the building was originally planned for. Some felt severely hampered by not enough work space, not enough office space, no storage room or closets, or by bad ventilation, or poor traffic control. Some colleges are operated on the approach that they had to have the students before they could get construction money; and in the meantime, they begged, borrowed, stole or rented space. Some new buildings required remodeling or rearrangement almost immediately, because the needs of the learners had changed so rapidly in programs offered while the building was under construction. Most administrators were planning on relatively limited, constantly weeded, active collections.

Remodeling of space and alterations was discussed by seventeen administrators. All but one felt that it was usually possible within a reasonable period, provided adequate groundwork and planning had been done. For one, it took almost a miracle; plans that had been approved locally were killed in the governor's office; sometimes the only approach was to slip it in piecemeal. Depending on the magnitude of the change wanted, the alteration might have required approval of a campus or district architect, various campus officials, or it might have been placed to wait its turn in a list of campus priorities. The waiting time might vary, therefore, from overnight to a year and a half. Usually a requisition or work order was required, then the plant manager or other engineer or architect investigated the feasibility and gave cost and time estimates. Often it had to have been something that the local staff was able to do, but their skills were often wide and very diversified.

Once the alteration had been approved, sometimes it was budgeted in the plant manager's budget, sometimes in the LRC's budget. Administrators stressed several factors: that a lot depended on the approach taken, that there had to be adequate understanding by the college administration, careful planning by the LRC staff, allowing enough lead time, and good interpersonal relationships with the plant manager and his staff. "If we can justify it, we can get it done." "How much they are able to do depends on what individual is asking." "I know what not to ask for--my president doesn't like anything that implies that the building was wrong."

GRANTS

A variety of federal and other grants had been received by the colleges interviewed. While four of the colleges reported that they had received almost no grant support, the majority had received Title II grants for materials, with at least the basic grant for most years. Other grants included Title III NDEA and Title VI for equipment. Eleven colleges reported grants of at least $40,000 over the last five year period, one as much as $225,000. Some specific projects for which grants were requested included Hispanic program (English as a second language), a microwave hookup with other institutions in the county, television, vocational education, Allied Health, and Afro-American studies.

Some campuses were much more militant grant-seekers than others. One campus had a college director of grants, seeking grants from a variety of public and private sources, and specializing in evaluating the educational effectiveness of the programs. Another LRC director always had a backlog file of special projects they would like to undertake.

Chapter 5

STAFF

Personnel expenditures accounted for about two-thirds of the learning resource budgets. Since this was the largest single expenditure in the budgets of all the learning resource departments, it became very important to analyze the organization, size, and type of personnel to account for this proportion of learning resource costs. In the twenty-seven campuses visited, personnel expenditures in 1972-73 ranged from $106,000 to $484,135; the mean was $286,232, the median $301,000. Staffs ranged in size from 13 to 60; the median size was 29.

STAFF ORGANIZATION

Twenty-two of the colleges were organized with the library and the audiovisual or media program as separate units within the college; although separate units, they might be within the same overall department, have a common administrative head, and share the same building. In addition to these two units, there were sometimes separate unit(s) for production services, and perhaps separate (central) technical processing. Fourteen of these units were headed by a common administrator of learning resources (also titled Dean of Learning Resources, Librarian, Dean of Library and Audiovisual Services, Director of Learning Resource Center, Director of the Library, Director of Educational Resources, Assistant Dean of Instructional Resources, Director, Division of Learning Resources, or Dean of Instructional Resources). Eight had no chief administrator for learning resources as such, although the librarian and the head of audio-visual services might have reported to a common general administrator, such as a Dean of Instruction.

In these twenty-two colleges, the library section followed generally conventional categories of Reference and Reader Advisement, Circulation, Periodicals, and Technical Services, including Acquisition and Cataloging. It was impossible to make a meaningful analysis of the number of personnel involved in each of these responsibilities, since people had overlapping duties, and a variety of assignments. In the fourteen colleges which had separate library and audiovisual departments under a common administrator, the library staff ranged in size from 6 to 31, the median size being 12. The Media Services, which were often split into at least two units, ranged in size from 6 to 24, the median size being 10. The combined staffs including administrators ranged from 19 to 59, the median size being 24.

In the eight colleges which had totally separate libraries and audiovisual services, the number in the two staffs ranged from 13 to 69, the median size being 28. The libraries ranged in size from 6 to 26, the median size being 14. The media service staffs ranged from 6 to 55, the median being 12.

The organization of these media services followed a wide variety of patterns; see Table 16:

-----Some were split by clientele served: faculty services, and individual student services

-----Some were split by function--distribution, learning laboratory, production by type, and innovation advisement

-----Some were split by facility for which each was responsible: for example, the language lab, the dial access lab, etc. Engineering was sometimes a separate subsection, or it was placed within distribution or production

-----Sometimes short production work was handled by one group, with long and major productions directed by another group

-----Often television production was a separate unit from other production; in some cases, this video production had its own engineers, graphic artists, and audio men, although there were sometimes separate units of each of these

In most media staffs of a dozen or fewer people, each had a variety of responsibilities and were able to perform in a variety of technical skill areas. It should also be understood that often in those libraries which were separate, some libraries serviced audiovisual materials; others even ran the principal wet media laboratory.

TABLE 16

MEDIA SERVICE STAFF ORGANIZATION IN 15 OF THE 22 COLLEGES HAVING SEPARATE LIBRARIES AND MEDIA SECTIONS

-----Media specialists, television technicians, projectionists, language lab technicians

-----Instructional Resources: Operations, engineering, booking

-----Instructional Resources: Management and booking, engineering, services and distribution
Production Development: Television; art, graphics and photography; film production

-----Educational Media Center:
Administration, booking and duplication
Production: photography, artists, television, audio
Distribution
Maintenance and development

-----Software and small production, learning laboratory;
Hardware; Large production and development

-----Instructional Media Services: Production service, classroom support, maintenance
Instructional Design: Educational applications of computer; Research and development

-----Media consultation, equipment maintenance, production, film booking, delivery service, television production and distribution

-----Booking, rentals and previews; graphic artist; technician

-----Media specialist for instructional development, graphics equipment delivery and setups, inventory control, repair

-----Scheduling, repair and maintenance, graphics-photography

-----Film and equipment services, AV materials production, audio and video production, photographic services, engineering support

-----Photography, scheduling films, AV cataloging, technician for grading papers in programmed learning lab, technician

-----Coordinator of Learning Laboratory
Coordinator of AV Services: production, equipment repair and installation; pickup delivery, and projection

-----Space Science Specialist
Multimedia Production Specialist
Audiovisual Supervisor: delivery of equipment, film library, maintenance

-----Educational television; developmental education; multi-media; audiovisual service and maintenance

Five learning resource centers visited were making every effort to give integrated service of both print and non-print materials--materials which were selected to serve the subject need of the user, regardless of format. In these learning resource centers, staff served by function in advisement, circulation and distribution, production, and instructional development. The staffs of these five learning resource centers ranged in size from 19 to 60, the median size being 36.

Each of these five learning resource centers had a somewhat different organizational structure:

-----Processing Service: Periodicals, acquisitions, cataloging
Resource Service: Reference and Media Specialists, circulation of both print and non-print, engineering
Production Services: Television, graphics, photography, audio

-----Design Production and Equipment: (hardware)
Selection, Acquisitions, Processing, includes periodicals and film booking

Distribution and Utilization: reference and circulation (software)

-----Materials Utilization and Production: Utilization consulting, design and graphics, audio, student media workshop, production consultation, photography and film, television and radio
Technical Processes and Materials Distribution: Circulation, distribution and repair, film booking, acquisitions, cataloging, processing, periodicals and bindery

-----Classroom Resources: Distribution, electronics, production
Center for Independent Study: Circulation and reference
Instructional Services: Resource consultation
Acquisition and Processing Services

-----Technical Services: Print and non-print acquisitions and cataloging
Instructional Technology: distribution and maintenance; presentation
Circulation
Media Specialists: Institute and general reference
Instructional Development Laboratory: Production
Print Shop

ADEQUACY AND NEEDS

As one would expect, there was very little correlation between size of staff, size per FTE student, and whether or not the staff thought that the staff was adequate. Further, different people within the staff often had radically different opinions about the adequacy of the staff. Some administrators tended to think that they were overstaffed, particularly in professionals. In some colleges there was marked difference in whether it was easier to get appropriations for professionals, technical assistants, or clericals--sometimes one harder, sometimes another. Some staffs had not grown in several years while the college had increased, and service was limited as a consequence. Areas differed in desirability; therefore, some administrators could pick and choose, while others considered recruiting difficult. Several administrators of inner-city campuses felt strongly that superior professionals were doubly essential in that environment, since it was more difficult to get good results with poorly prepared or less motivated students. Some administrators felt a disproportionately high percentage of their budgets went into salaries, because of vigorous negotiating by staff groups. Several administrators expressed the philosophy that the most successful administrative style was to let people do what they wanted. Their rationale was that "you never can do everything, it all produces good results, and people are happier and perform better if they are doing what they like."

Of the unbudgeted positions that administrators wished to add, graphic artists and audio technicians ("well-rounded, multi-skilled, adjustable, calm and unruffled") were among the most often expressed. A few middle level section heads frankly said that their problems with personnel were not with the number of warm bodies, but with the quality of those they had; if all had been top-notch performers, they felt that the size would probably have been adequate.

Opinion differed widely on the usefulness of work study assistants and student aides. Some administrators were obviously doing a superb job of in-service training, including not only job skills, but discipline, motivation, and commitment. They stated that it was constant effort, but they seemed to have the administrative skill to control effectively without resentment. Many other administrators on all levels were not successful with their student workers and very much wanted to replace them with regular staff.

Three factors--the overall morale of the staff, their feelings about whether their efforts were appreciated, and their faith and trust in their chief--seemed to have effected large differences in accomplishment levels in relationship to the size of the staff.

The actual amount of instructional development varied widely from campus to campus; perhaps this was the area requiring the greatest interpersonal skill and rapport. Administrators differed in their assessment of how successful they thought their staffs were in this area, and in their descriptions of what to look for in recruiting for this kind of work with faculty and students.

Directors from time to time spoke wistfully of their own need for a reliable administrative assistant to carry through on projects, do trouble shooting and take care of routines.

Colleges differed widely on whether the salary scales were competitive with those found locally, especially for clerical and technical groups. In many schools promotion guidelines for LRC personnel were the same as those for teaching faculty. One administrator said, "I have problems with my administration because the reference staff doesn't always look like they're working."

Since the colleges differed widely as to age, so did the number of years of service of the staffs; some of the older colleges, for instance, reported very stable staffs, most of whom had been with the college long periods.

"Most of them probably feel overworked; I believe in keeping people hopping; they perform better."

Strong need was expressed in some Learning Resource departments for good script writers, a relatively new area. This correlated with the emphasis on individualized, custom-made instructional materials, which often required extensive script writing.

Increased emphasis on Affirmative Action had lead to tightening of recruiting practices in most places, with far more careful advertising, documentation, resumes of conferences and interviews, guidelines for final selection, and far more investigation of prior work experience and academic qualifications. Some colleges seemed to have significant discrepancies in qualification and rank classification of technical staff ; because of the local situation, or because the LRC ran its own TA program, administrators were able to hire people with a high degree of training at clerical rates. Similarly, in a few areas, the market for bachelor degree audiovisual people was glutted, and colleges were able to hire them at technical assistant or clerical pay scales. In some respects this could produce excellent results, but it was not without morale problems.

The emphasis on production of custom-designed materials for instructors and students was one of the most important differences in emphasis between the community college learning resource center and the traditional library in four year colleges and universities. For this reason, it would have been extremely useful to know how much staff time and therefore, what proportion of the personnel budget was actually going into production. Estimating this amount of production time was almost impossible, however, because almost all the distribution staff became involved in production at some point, and even the reference staff at times did. Nevertheless, an attempt was made to estimate how many people in the twenty-seven campuses had production as their primary responsibility. The range was zero to thirty; the median was 4. These figures are skewed somewhat by one production staff of 30 for a district being housed on one of its campuses.

Most of the staffs were hierarchically organized; however, there were four LRC's within which all professionals reported directly to the director.

PROFESSIONAL/CLERICAL RATIO

The ratio of number of professional staff to number of clerical staff differed widely in the twenty-seven colleges visited, and often differed from section to section within the libraries and audiovisual departments within a particular college. Ratios ranged from 3:1 professional/clerical to 2:7 professional/clerical. Further, there was some expressed satisfaction and some dissatisfaction at almost every level of ratio. More than half the library and the media directors thought that a ratio of 1 to 2 was about right, but five administrators thought 1 to 3 or 4 was better. In part this difference might have been due to differences in definition: whether or not the semi-professional or technical assistants were included with the professional or with the clerical. In some states the so-called "classified" category of personnel (as opposed to the "Certificated" or faculty-rank master's level or above) covered a very wide range of training, experience, responsibility and salary.

Not all administrators recognized the economy of having a sufficient number of trained typists for reference and bibliography staffs, graphics staffs, and script typists for production. Failure to achieve optimum ratios could result in using either professional or typist groups poorly and reducing the benefit of the salary expenditure.

Chapter 6

FACULTY, STUDENT, AND LEARNING RESOURCE STAFF INTERRELATIONSHIPS

As a group, learning resource staff in community colleges were highly service oriented, they were almost evangelically geared toward increasing the use of print and non-print materials among faculty and students, and they tried very hard to help this process however they could.

STAFF AND FACULTY INTERACTION

Since most learning resource staff felt that the main key to student use was faculty expectation and requirement, they employed a variety of means to convince the faculty of the value of using learning resource materials.

Most learning resource administrators thought it was good to have their staffs serve as actively as possible on faculty senates, faculty associations and clubs and faculty committees of all kinds, but especially on curriculum committees. The administrators stressed the importance of staff members being articulate participants, concerned and knowledgeable about the instructional problems of their colleagues.

Most learning resource staffs made a deliberate effort to regularly attend department and divisional meetings with the teaching faculty, to learn what plans were being made, and to make suggestions for using resources in the solution of educational problems. Many learning resource departments assign specific people to specific departments, in order that they might get to know each other better, and could intensively be responsible for the resources in that subject area. However, some LRC's felt that formalizing responsibility to a specific faculty had disadvantages, and that a rotating system attempting to know all was better; it depended on the size of the faculty, and particularly on the size of the professional staff.

Many campuses had a library and/or learning resources faculty committee, whose responsibilities varied widely. They might have some authority in the allocation of materials funds, might assist in establishment of production priorities, or might merely be a sounding board for the convenience of the LRC administrator.

On one campus, a member of the learning resources staff was the elected faculty representative on the Board of Trustees; this was very helpful not only in presenting the learning resource viewpoint and helping to educate the Trustees, but also in developing broad acquaintance with the teaching program.

Most of the learning resource departments participated actively in the orientation programs for their faculty, both the general ones sponsored by the college administrations and special ones that they gave on their own. These covered a variety of approaches, letting the faculty know what was available and what the LRC could do for them. In one college workshop, the faculty were required to develop an AV presentation that they had designed, scripted, and helped to produce. Some colleges held the entire orientation in the library because they benefited from the relaxed, comfortable atmosphere. Variety in these presentations was important; faculty did not want to hear the same thing year after year. Having the faculty as active, not merely listening and looking, participants was important. Some LRC staff were particularly successful in building rapport with faculty by previewing films with them, since the faculty member's response could be very informative beyond his reaction to that particular film.

In order to get the faculty into a more active role between the student and the materials, one LRC had developed a special program called PROJECT PENCIL, "Practically Everybody Needs Counseling In Library." Project PENCIL scheduled volunteer faculty on a regular basis to spend certain hours in the library every week, working with students in using materials. A desk for the faculty was in the middle of the reference area. The faculty member received no formal training except an orientation on where things were. The faculty member was responsible for helping with subject information in the broad area of his competence; usually, he had told his own classes, and often his department's what hours he was scheduled. The reference staff continued to answer general informational questions, and to give one-to-one instruction in use of materials; but the faculty and LRC staff often became involved in a team teaching process. One comment seemed to sum up the attitude of the staff: "It works well."

Another way two campuses had gotten their faculties actively involved was by giving them a responsible role not only in selection, but in weeding the collection. "All the faculty are assigned certain sections to read shelves and shelf lists regularly to review the collection for gaps and for removing obsolete materials."

"Not all our faculty have adequate offices, so we keep a faculty room where they can come for quiet work."

Nevertheless, some libraries still took the approach of not getting out to the facuty, but of sending them material and asking the faculty to come to them. Faculty handbooks, newsletters, new book lists, CHOICE cards, materials blurbs, lists of holdings in their area, periodicals lists, welcoming letters, and a quarterly library bulletin were among these approaches. Two media directors volunteered the opinion that the reason the media program was so much better supported by the faculty than the library program was that, "Library staff don't get out of the library enough. They should go out and sell more, not wait for people to come to them."

Over and over directors of dynamic programs stressed the importance of the whole staff's getting out and selling service to faculty and students. "Socialize; I know every faculty member on campus by his first name, most of them well." "Be casual and informal; soft sell works best; be helpful and friendly and non-threatening." "Solicit service, then be sure your crew delivers; don't overcommit." "Promotion is a major responsibility." "Woo them; suggest, don't bludgeon; they don't need the library, I need them." What proportion of staff time was spent outside the center varied widely. In one campus the proportions were 90%, 50%, and 40% of the time of the three top LRC personnel. In another campus it was one-third of the professional time, across the board. In another ten hours per week per person, on a fairly regular schedule; this campus had provided a second office for the LRC staff members within the teaching faculty office cluster; "We've come a long way."

In at least four of the campuses, LRC staff were regularly assigned as part of the teaching team, in several capacities: the development of materials, the provision of information, and direct instruction.

Some learning resource departments organized their staff primarily on the basis of who works with whom; for example, the Audiovisual Services unit might primarily work with faculty, including production and distribution of equipment, while the learning resource center might primarily work with students.

FACULTY ATTITUDES TOWARD MEDIA

Faculty attitudes toward the use of media in instruction were considered to be of major importance in the success or failure of the learning resources program. For the most part, the faculty determined whether or not students actually used materials, either print or nonprint. In most instances administrative support for the use of media was helpful; about one-fourth of the learning resource administrators felt they had strong backing from their administrations in pushing use of media with the faculty. In a few schools, agreement to use media was part of the contract which faculty members signed. Occasionally this pressure from administrations had backfired into faculty resentment. Ten LRC administrators indicated that they thought the faculty attitude toward using media was very good. "About 90% of the faculty use." "Attitude very good--use continually and heavily." "We are the leaders in this district, the showplace; and the faculty are aware of it, and use is steadily growing on campus. "Enthusiastic." "Friendly, warm, nice feeling throughout; we recruit for business subtly." "Faculty is receptive; there was initial fear, but those we worked with spread the message." "The way to get them is to go out and talk individually, and develop faculty interest geared to them; talk about their needs and objectives; act as salesmen; we see a high percentage each term. You have to work at it."

On the other hand, at least nine administrators thought the prevailing attitude was negative. "We don't get either top administrative or divisional support, so most of the faculty take a hands-off position." "The College is anti-media." "It's only lip service interest in mediated approach." "Faculty are afraid if they produce or use programs they will be replaced." "At best it is a crutch for faculty, not a well-planned part of instruction." "We have no organized effort to inform the faculty, and their lack of utilization may be the result of their not knowing what we have or what we can do." "We are having an uphill fight for acceptance; have to remedy our reliability image." "Faculty complain about having to innovate." "In the budget crunch we had to discontinue pick-up and delivery; it hurt us badly; bad decreases in usage."

Most administrators felt that good service and helpful attitudes were the keys to increased usage. "If you give good service they can rely on, your requests will always exceed what you can provide." "Before the community colleges separated from the district, media use was actually discouraged; since then it has increased twentyfold. Our department was hired to build a positive image."

LRC's were using both formal and informal methods of instructing faculty in use of media. Most agreed that informal one-to-one dialog was the most effective, but many also had workshops and orientation sessions. Sometimes those workshops were limited to use of equipment; others stressed use of media to meet educational objectives, including selection, preparation, and evaluation; still others included demonstrations and hands-on sessions with faculty for faculty preparation of media materials. It was considered to be extremely important that the approach to in-service training be relevant to the faculty, not just an explanation of LRC procedures. Response apparently varied widely: some administrators said that only two or three people showed up for scheduled in-service training. Another said that the LRC staff had announced a two day spring workshop on video-graphics, and the use of equipment, expecting a maximum of twenty; however, faculty demand was so great that they had to spread the sessions to four half-day workshops. Usually the very popular centers were those where faculty could have production equipment available, especially if there were a technician there to show them how to use it. At a minimum these usually included a photocopier, primary typewriter, transparency maker, and often slide-making equipment and a recording booth.

Other ways of getting the message to faculty included handbooks, current awareness lists and newsletter, film catalogs, and departmental preview sessions.

In at least four of the community colleges, LRC faculty taught courses that the teaching faculty could use to update or renew their certificates. Television production courses seemed to be particularly popular.

LIBRARIANS' ATTITUDES TO NON-PRINT

In the twenty-two campuses where the library was a separate unit, librarians' attitudes varied widely with regard to non-print material and their responsibilities in the non-print field.

Audio services seemed to be popular; phonodisc or tape collections and wet carrels for listening were part of the services of almost all libraries. In the visual area, however, at least a quarter of the libraries either had no film and graphics materials, or were just beginning to collect them. Slide collections, though, were often of significant size. Some of the libraries had the entire range of college.

owned non-print materials available for student use, including purchased media as well as that which they had produced for individual study. Motion picture showing for students and/or video cassettes were available to students in only a few of the libraries. Some libraries circulated cassettes and even cassette players for home use. Some libraries controlled especially equipped learning laboratories where materials, guidance, and equipment were available to students; other libraries scattered the wet carrels around the stacks. Some libraries publicized weekly what films were on campus what days on a rental basis, and encouraged as broad individual and classroom usage as possible. One campus had a Open Cinema where all rented films were video distributed, and students could relax around the third floor Pad and watch.

Several library directors thought that more of the non-print facilities should be under their direction; but when questioned about the extent of their commitment, they seemed reluctant to spend the money or staff time necessary for a dynamic program. Some library staff expressed outright resentment at the amounts of money being spent on their campuses for various media programs. Intershelving of print and non-print material was discussed wistfully by some librarians but mentioned with dread or abhorrence by others; it was actually in successful operation in two of the learning resource centers.

When the media and the library staffs were separate, the amount of cooperation between them varied from almost none to very high. In some places, neither knew what the other had, or what they were doing; each program went its separate way. In other places regular weekly or bi-weekly meetings for information and discussion were held, and "Good rapport and very practical cooperation exists between the two groups;

it's a nice place to work, the esprit de corps is very high."

Relatively few of the librarians had had formal courses in media, or the media staff in work with print material. On three campuses, deliberate effort was being made to improve this proportion. One staff was having a two hour weekly orientation to the full range of resources.

ATTITUDES ON SERVICE TO STUDENTS

Most LRC staff felt strongly that there was a high commitment, backed up by steady, hard effort, to provide outgoing service to students. Although the service attitude might vary from staff member to staff member, most of the staff were ready to give a lot of direct help, to direct and even to spoon feed, if necessary. Since many community college students were not articulate about what they wanted, a special effort had to be made to find out exactly what his assignment was, interpret it for him, and guide him in its completion. "Stick with him." Although staff hoped that the student would eventually become independent, they recognized that the persistence and follow through ability of many of these students was not very high. Staff members generally felt that the students needed to be led, step by step, with short, specific directions, and as few optional suggestions as necessary to avoid confusion. "They don't get into books easily; reading is not a way of life for them; you have to study the kind of student they are, what they can absorb, and how receptive they are." "Staff have to be attuned to various types of students; they vary widely in what they will do on their own; some come in with a chip on their shoulder, and we turn them around."

Some of the learning centers were making a very deliberate attempt to make the place appealing both to the students, physically and psychologically, using unconventional means, if necessary. Live lectures, contemporary music, TV while studying, snack bars, smoking areas, lounge furniture, and stereo were all used to get and keep the students in the LRC building. "They know they can get help; they're not in awe when they come in; it's a nice place to spend time."

Chapter 7

STUDENT UTILIZATION OF MATERIALS AND FACILITIES

The amount of use students gave the materials and facilities varied widely. One LRC with over a thousand seats claimed it was often completely full on all floors. "We're overused; we are so crowded that both students and staff suffer." In direct contrast, some libraries were mostly empty except for a few hours a day. While most librarians encouraged the use of the facility for recreational purposes, several were pleased that as the college got older, the library was used less for a study hall, and more as a resource facility. "We're steadily busy; usually buzzing. People are waiting for service, and we have to learn to juggle several readers at once; it's very important, nevertheless, to give the impression of accessibility." Some reported that there was heavy use of the main learning resource building, but much less use of the special learning spaces in other buildings.

At least a third of the learning resource centers reported that their rate of use was increasing every year, and that it was going up proportionally faster than the increase in enrollment. On the other hand, at least three schools reported that there had been sharp drops in circulation and building use when enrollment dropped, and a fourth said its usage had declined sharper than the decrease in FTE. Some librarians thought that decreasing use of materials was due to fewer term paper assignments as the college had increased individual class sizes. Most tried for as liberal a circulation policy as possible. More use within the building, more use by instructors of paperbacks and reprints, and less emphasis on reserve books, resulted in a change in many loan periods to one, three and seven day collections. Several librarians stated that they felt their students were working more in depth, and more independently. Several librarians commented that they kept statistics on number of books and periodicals reshelved from the tables; they felt this indicated that there was very heavy in-house use of materials, increasing in volume annually. In some places, however, the tendency of students was to take home rather than to use materials at the LRC.

Few of the libraries had statistics on how much of the collection was actually being used. One that did receive this information item by item each semester, found that the proportion used was high, well over a third of the holdings.

In one learning resource center, the circulation of non-print materials was far higher--two or three to one--than the print. One LRC administrator said that circulation and usage had doubled since moving into a new building two years ago. "We hope we're never satisfied." One LRC said that their college systems approach created high use of instructional packages, but not much use of the general collection; the packages had been designed to be self-sufficient.

CIRCULATION STATISTICS

The Guide to Methods of Library Evaluation developed by the Association of College and Research Libraries, Committee on Liaison with Accrediting Agencies (ALA, 1968, p. 297), states:

> The use the students make of the library is the ultimate test of its effectiveness and is the result of various library conditions and faculty teaching methods. Significance may be found in the extent of student use of reading spaces, the quality of reference

> service asked of librarians, and the size of annual circulation volume for the reserve and general collections. Insight may also be gained by questioning a selection of students on the character of their use.

Nevertheless, many valid objections were raised concerning the use of circulation statistics as comparative measures of library effectiveness. One librarian said, "I could double the circulation tomorrow by closing the periodical stacks and counting every time I handed out a magazine, but I would be disservicing our readers." Several factors affected circulation statistics: How many faculty assigned reserve reading, the number of duplicate copies available to large classes, the frequency of term papers, the availability of other strong libraries nearby, the traffic patterns on campus, and the relative amount of money students had to spend on buying material and making photocopies. However, data on circulation were one of the few specific measures of usage that have been developed for libraries; therefore, statistics were kept by most.

Circulation statistics were kept in a number of categories: books, reserves, periodicals, discs, tapes, 16mm films, pamphlets, various AV software, interlibrary loans, microforms, occasionally hardware (although this was usually kept separately from statistics on content materials), and occasionally, the number of photocopies made. Many libraries keep circulation records by groups within the subject classification.

Comprehensive circulation figures were available for twenty-four of the campuses visited. These ranged from 7,726 to 138,000; the mean was 60,600 and the median was 52,000. The circulation per FTE student ranged from 3.35 to 23.76; the aggregate mean was 9.58, the mean averaged from the separate campus statistics was 9.83, and the median was 8.94. The mean for those learning resource centers where print and non-print were integrated was 13.14; the mean for those campuses where the library was a separate unit was 9.16.

This FTE circulation figure was analyzed by how old the campus was, the expenditure per FTE for total learning resources, for print materials, for staff, and the size of the book collection, as shown in Tables 17-21. Table 17 shows no discernable pattern between the date the campus was established and the circulation per FTE; in order to evaluate whether aggregate usage per FTE had indeed increased faster than enrollment, the historical statistics on each campus would have to be plotted. Nor was there a significant correlation between FTE circulation and any of the four other variables plotted. In analyzing the relationship between total learning resource expenditure, only those fourteen campuses were used (out of the 16 discussed in Chapter 3) for which both full budgets and comprehensive circulation figures were available.

TABLE 17

ANNUAL CIRCULATION PER FTE STUDENT
BY DATE LRC WAS ESTABLISHED

annual circulation per FTE student	Date LRC was Established					
	Before 1940	1946 to 1959	1960 to 1964	1965 to 1969	1970 to 1973	Row Totals
4 or under			1	3	1	5
5 - 7	2		2	2		6
8 - 10	1	1	1	1	1	5
11 - 13	1		1			2
14 - 16		1		1		2
17 - 19		1				1
20 or over			1	1		2
Column Totals	4	3	6	8	2	23

TABLE 18

ANNUAL CIRCULATION PER FTE STUDENT
AND SIZE OF BOOK COLLECTION

annual circulation per FTE student	Size of Book Collection in Volumes							
	20,000-39,999	40,000-59,999	60,000-79,999	80,000-99,999	100,000-119,999	120,000-139,999	140,000 or over	Row Totals
4 or under	2	2	1					5
5 - 7		3	1		1		1	6
8 - 10	1	2	1	1				5
11 - 13			1		1			2
14 - 16				2				2
17 - 19		1						1
20 or over	1	1						2
Column Totals	4	9	4	3	2		1	23

TABLE 19

ANNUAL CIRCULATION PER FTE STUDENT
BY EXPENDITURE PER FTE FOR
LEARNING RESOURCES (14 CAMPUSES)

annual circulation per FTE student	Expenditure per FTE for Learning Resources									
	25-49	50-74	75-99	100-124	125-149	150-174	175-199	200-224	225 and over	Row Totals
4 or under	1		1				1			3
5 - 7	1		1							2
8 - 10	1	2	1							4
11 - 13			1	1						2
14 - 16				1	1					2
17 - 19										
20 or over									1	1
Column Totals	3	2	4	2	1		1		1	14

TABLE 20

ANNUAL CIRCULATION PER FTE STUDENT
BY PRINT MATERIAL EXPENDITURE
PER FTE (14 CAMPUSES)

annual circulation per FTE student	Print Material Expenditure per FTE					
	$4-6.99	$7-9.99	$10-12.99	$13-15.99	$16 and over	Row Totals
4 or under		1	2			3
5 - 7	2					2
8 - 10			4			4
11 - 13			1		1	2
14 - 16	1				1	2
17 - 19						
20 or over			1			1
Column Totals	3	1	8		2	14

TABLE 21

ANNUAL CIRCULATION PER FTE STUDENT
BY PERSONNEL EXPENDITURE PER
FTE STUDENT (14 CAMPUSES)

annual circulation per FTE student	Personnel Expenditure per FTE Student					
	Under $25	$25-49	$50-74	$75-99	$100-124	Row Totals
4 or under	1	1			1	3
5 - 7	1			1		2
8 - 10		1	3			4
11 - 13		2				2
14 - 16		1		1		2
17 - 19						
20 or over					1	1
Column Totals	2	5	3	2	2	14

ATTENDANCE STATISTICS

As many valid objections to using attendance counts for comparative purposes could be raised as objections to using circulation figures. Students might not have come into the learning resource center to use it for its primary purpose at all, but to use the telephone, to meet someone, or for some other purpose. The LRC might be a convenient traffic path to somewhere else. Classes might meet in the LRC. Turnstiles count staff and student aides who come in and out. The LRC might be the only place on campus where students could sit, or get out of the cold; this pattern might change radically upon completion of a new student center. Attendance might vary with moving into a new building.

Turnstile counts or counts by door attendants were available from twelve of the campuses visited. The range was 69,000 to 692,000; the mean 305,410, the median 274,000. The range in attendance per FTE student was 9.63 to 62.51; the mean was 42.93, the median 50.23. Of those learning resource centers where print and non-print services were integrated, the mean attendance was 31.10; in the others where the library was a separate unit, the mean attendance was 46.87.

No significant correlation or pattern was found between attendance per FTE and size of book collection, age of the campus, or FTE expenditure for total learning resources, print materials, or staff.

The comparison between FTE attendance and FTE circulation is shown in Table 22. There was a slight tendency for circulation to increase as attendance increased. Statistics for both attendance and circulation were available for only eleven campuses.

TABLE 22

ANNUAL ATTENDANCE PER FTE STUDENT BY
ANNUAL CIRCULATION PER FTE STUDENT

annual circulation per FTE student	Annual Attendance per FTE student						
	Under 20	20-29	30-39	40-49	50-59	60 or over	Row Totals
4 or under					1		1
5 - 7	1						1
8 - 10	1		2	1	1		5
11 - 13						1	1
14 - 16					1	1	2
17 - 19						1	1
Column Totals	2		2	1	3	3	11

CIRCULATION METHODS

Nine of the campuses had a single circulation desk for all library materials; fourteen had two desks; three had three desks; and one had six desks. The number of desks might depend on the number of floors in the library or the number of exits. Where there were two desks, the split was some combination of: general, reserve, media, periodicals, microforms, or 16mm films.

Nine of the campuses used an off-line computer data processing system for circulation and one campus had been on-line since September. Most of them received a daily report listing all outstanding material by call number and by student number, often social security number. Some campuses also received reports by author or title. Some of these nine libraries included only print materials in the automated system, but two libraries included non-print material as well. Reports varied on the amount of downtime experienced with the data processing equipment. Regular computer-produced overdues, and much more elaborate statistics on usage were usually part of these computer programs.

Eight campuses used Brodart SYSTAC circulation systems. Two used Gaylord charge plates. One of the campuses did not have prepared book cards; each time a borrower wanted to take out an item, he had to write out in full the author, title, and call number. One campus used Keysort cards. The rest used conventional book card systems that the students signed.

CLOSED STACKS

Various learning resource collections on various campuses were housed in closed stacks and paged for users on request. All but one of the campuses had collections of closed reserve books put on reserve at the request of faculty for assignment to classes; in some campuses, these materials were print only, in others it included all formats. Other types of materials that were in closed stacks were:

All AV software - 5 campuses
Tapes and cassettes - 2 campuses
16mm films - 3 campuses
Self-instructional materials - 1 campus
Video cassettes - 1 campus
College catalogs - 1 campus

Three campuses routinely put on closed reserve those materials from the general collection that were frequently stolen; this included subject areas such as: sex, karate, automobile mechanics, nursing materials, and police science materials.

PERIODICALS

The number of periodicals received ranged from about 200 to over 3000 titles, the median was about 650. About half the campuses had closed periodical stacks, although this might vary depending on whether the journal was bound or unbound. About a third of the campuses permitted overnight or short-term borrowing of periodicals. Most of the campuses did little or no binding of journals; periodicals were discarded, or kept on microforms, or sent to a central pool with daily delivery on request to campuses; three campuses did extensive in-house adhesive binding. Some campuses said they had very little problem with theft and mutilation; in some campuses the problems were extensive. Most campuses issued an annual title and subject list of their periodicals and distributed the list to their faculty.

THEFT CONTROL

Eight of the campuses had installed surveillance systems (three different systems) to reduce loss of material. Most of them were very satisfied, and all reported significant reductions in loss. Four other campuses very much hoped to install security devices, were investigating systems, and were trying to get appropriations. Two campuses used door attendants to check all users as they exited.

Security of equipment was a severe problem in some campuses; others had little or no problem. Permanent equipment installed in classrooms or lecture halls was a special problem.

Constant attention was repeatedly named as the only remedy for equipment loss. "We keep extremely careful theft control, and have lost nothing except one mike in four years. Although we turn the keys over to students for overnight, we constantly work at security, and never take anything for granted. Everything is locked within rooms, not just doors. Everybody signs in and out; no unauthorized personnel are allowed in; we enforce stringently keeping the traffic down. We impress on all personnel and all students when they are hired that they are never to turn their back on the equipment and never leave it; there is a student with each piece at all times. The security office knows we try, and they reinforce. We have no money for replacements; if we lose something, we have to stay without."

EXTENDED CIRCULATION SERVICES

Several of the campuses had extended circulation services of significant volume. One campus circulated almost a thousand items to county residents not enrolled as students. Some campuses had active interlibrary loan programs with neighboring libraries, often including reciprocal borrowing.

Some campuses made a special effort to serve the students attending classes in satellite campuses of the college. One of these served sixty locations by means of a shuttle bus carrying materials. Another had assigned staff to work intensively with the students in the Senior Citizens Center and another to work with the Black and Chicano students in off-campus locations.

HOURS

Library or Learning Resource Center hours varied. Schedules of opening hours were collected for twenty-three campuses. The Monday through Thursday schedule was:

7 a.m.-9:45 p.m.	4	8 a.m.-10:00 p.m.	4	8 a.m.- 8:30 p.m.	1
7:30 -10:00 p.m.	5	8 a.m.- 9:30 p.m.	1	8 a.m.- 3:30 p.m.	1
7:45 -10:00 p.m.	5	8 a.m.- 9:00 p.m.	1	8:30 -10:00 p.m.	1

Sixteen of the libraries closed at 5:00 p.m. on Fridays, one at 4:00 p.m., and one at 6:00 p.m. Ten libraries were open only in the mornings on Saturday; two were open only in the afternoon; five were open all day; and six did not open at all on Saturday. Eight libraries opened four hours on Sunday afternoons; one library was open from 2:30 p.m. to 10:00 p.m. on Sunday afternoon.

Weekly hours open ranged from 46 to 74. The mean was 69.6, the median was 71, and the mode 73 (30%).

Chapter 8

READER SERVICES

Most of the wide range of reader services that have been developed in libraries were offered by one or another of the community college resource departments. Some were much more active than others; size of staff available for reference and reader services per FTE varied widely.

INSTRUCTING STUDENTS IN USE OF MATERIALS

Most of the libraries make an effort to instruct the students in use of materials, including, usually, the use of the card catalog and indexes, and location of materials. Six of the campuses had courses required of all entering students; three of these were class taught, three were packaged self instruction. Seven other campuses had courses that were elective, which varied from one to three credits. Nine campuses gave library instruction through the English department; some of these covered as many as 100 sections. Eighteen libraries reported that they also gave special subject instruction in bibliography to specific groups on request; these included a wide range of subjects, such as Engineering, Dental, Business, Nursing, Sewerage Treatment, Hotel/Motel, Law, and Construction Technology; the numbers of these special lectures given per year varied:

Under 20	- 2	40 - 59	- 3	100 - 150	- 4
20 - 39	- 4	60 - 79	- 3	200 - 300	- 2

Library staffs had prepared, usually with the help of the production staff, a variety of media aids for this instruction in use of the library. Thirteen had prepared slide-tape shows; two had produced 16mm films in color; one had done a videotape; and seven had walking tours self-guided with diagrams for use with cassette players and headsets. Five others used live tours; their estimates of what proportion of the students took the tour were: "most," "at least 80%," 60%, 10%, and "about 50" students.

REFERENCE SERVICES

Most libraries tried to schedule coverage at the reference desk at all times; many of them tried to cover always with a professional; some libraries had several desks located at strategic points; in some libraries all the professionals, regardless of their primary assignment, took turns at the reference desk.

Reference staffs performed a variety of special services. Most of them prepared bibliographies from time to time, of three types: general handout bibliographies on topics of current interest geared to student non-course use; course-related bibliographies, which often included non-print materials; bibliographies for faculty in areas of their research. Sometimes they were able to do extensive literature searches for faculty; one staff regularly provided assistance to faculty in writing dissertation and grant proposals and in compiling related bibliographies. Most campuses would obtain materials for both faculty and students on interlibrary loan. Two campuses photocopied tables of contents of incoming journals and sent them to interested faculty as a current awareness service; others listed incoming cataloged material in the field of the faculty member's interest. One campus offered a special service to students in reading their term papers and helping them make corrections in form and language. Most libraries prepared exhibits from time to time.

Career information collections were maintained for students by several libraries; some had assigned a special room to this collection. One library maintained two special clipping files: biographical information on authors for book reports and a file of clippings by subject from local newspapers. Special indexing projects included periodical articles on their state and local area, and materials on criminal justice. Oral history and college archives projects have been undertaken by several campuses.

One campus had instituted a home delivery system of materials, with the cooperation of community agencies. Another was aiding a program of cooperation between the college and industry. One learning resource director was responsible for summarizing and channeling the student evaluations of instructors, and of reviewing text book selections.

At least five of the campuses included formal counseling-personal, academic, career, and financial-among the responsibilities of the learning resource department. Formal counseling on study skills was handled in a variety of ways. One center worked intensively in alternative presentations of the subject matter, texts, and special materials; they stressed reading, vocabulary, spelling, and mathematics skills, study techniques, and development with the faculty of minicourses for problem areas. Their approach was non-punitive and geared to the average student, not just the poor students; the students felt that the presentations carried no stigma.

TECHNICAL ASSISTANT CURRICULUMS

Nine of the campuses offered two-year training programs with degree credit for technical assistants. No attempt was made to investigate these programs in this survey.

PHOTOCOPYING AND COPYRIGHT

There was some kind of photocopying machine, usually self-service, on every campus. Most made no effort to control its use by either faculty or students; but one campus did restrict faculty to five copies, not enough to hand out to classes; another asked faculty to get reprints.

Eight centers would dub cassettes for students; several college bookstores carried blank cassettes for this purpose.

One campus made it a practice to videotape a number of expensive film rentals. Another videotaped the film only if the film arrived late and had to be sent back, and only for the showing for which the rental was paid.

Copying of radio programs and phonodics played over the air had been done widely in some places. One director said, "Taping off the air is in the public domain." Another said their campus had over 5000 audiotapes made illegally off the air, but he did not make college policy. Another center had a carefully developed plan for recording audio and video programs off the air: They recorded both the program and the commercials, then wrote to the sponsor that they would play back with commercials for educational purposes only, and that this would increase the sponsor's audience range. Response was usually good; if not, the tape was wiped. Another campus had found that if they stated that use would be for classroom distribution only, it was usually possible to get releases.

Copyright attitudes varied from indifference to earnest attempt not to break the law, not to reproduce pictures from books,"We decided to do the safe thing," to admitted lip service "Don't get caught," "We've discussed, but keep on doing."

Chapter 9

SELECTION OF MATERIALS, TECHNICAL SERVICES, AND COMPUTER APPLICATIONS

All learning resource staff felt a high responsibility toward acquisition of appropriate materials, of as high a quality as their users could utilize with benefit. Usually this was a shared responsibility, and most directors worked at seeing that the sharing was as broadly based as possible.

SELECTION OF PRINT MATERIALS

While books, periodicals, and other materials were selected by both faculty and staff in all institutions, the ratios varied widely, and the amount of emphasis that the library director placed in achieving faculty participation varied also. Some worked very hard to get as many faculty as possible to participate; others wanted to work through department chairmen or division heads only. Usually all professional library staff had responsibilities for selection, often designated by specific competence. Estimates of the proportion of print materials selected by faculty and staff were:

Faculty:	Staff:	Number of campuses:
90%	10%	1
80	20	1
70	30	1
50	50	3
40	60	2
30	70	1
10	90	4

Most directors said they did not censor faculty requests, although they might discuss some of them. On some campuses, faculty requests required the department chairman or division head's approval. Eleven of the campuses allocated their materials budget by department, and sent the department a regular accounting of the amount spent and outstanding; one of these reports listed materials by title, and provided detailed statistics on discounts, date of receipt and balance. Sometimes this allocation was based strictly on enrollment; sometimes the basis was an estimate of the proportion of the subject market and relative price in that discipline.

Most libraries regularly sent material to faculty asking them if they were interested in particular titles; publishers' blurbs, reviews, _Library Journal_ reviews, and _Choice_ cards were frequently mentioned.

Three learning resource staffs had developed extensive manuals for their own and faculty use on selection policy and procedures. Relatively few campuses made any attempt to preview print material before purchase, and approval plans were mentioned by only two.

SELECTION OF NON-PRINT MATERIALS

In contrast, non-print material was usually previewed before purchase whenever possible. Staff and administrators recognized that this was a very time-consuming process, and that careful track had to be kept of the status and location of material brought in for preview. Common practice involved the media center's maintaining a file of bibliographies, catalogs, blurbs, and other materials on media; a faculty member would tell the staff what subject coverage he needed; and a subject search would be made. The faculty member would review the findings of this search and select the things he wanted to preview. When the material arrived, he would look at it, often together with a staff member; wherever possible, departmental consensus on the material would be sought. Formal evaluation sheets done by the previewers were usually kept on file whether or not the material was purchased.

Funding of non-print media was even more complicated than print media. About a third of the campuses allocated non-print materials budgets by department. In six campuses these materials were charged back to the budget of the instructional department; and in four campuses, the materials were physically sent to the department for permanent retention. Some of the justification reports on purchase of materials were very detailed, and included: full bibliographic information, number of faculty voting on the acquisition; number who previewed the material; estimate of the number of classroom showings per term, and the number of students involved; and cost of rental or special conditions.

ACQUISITIONS

Although most libraries placed their orders for print materials directly, some went through a central purchasing department, district, college, or city/county, as discussed in the section on purchasing. Four campuses and district acquisitions departments were using computer-produced orders. To get around the problem of having to cancel orders not received by a cutoff date, or of having to bid materials, nine campuses routinely issued blanket purchase orders to their major vendors, and ordered against these blanket orders. These were not, in essence, a commitment by title, but merely a credit to buy against; some of these open purchase orders were issued under annual contracts. One librarian felt strongly that his method of buying directly from publishers rather than jobbers saved an average of six weeks per title delivery time.

It was arbitrarily decided at the beginning of the survey that there was not sufficient time to permit meaningful analyses of procedures in technical services, either acquisition or cataloging. Therefore, in most cases, personnel in these areas were not interviewed. However, two district technical services offices were observed in detail.

CATALOGING

About a quarter of the campuses visited were still buying a high proportion of their materials preprocessed and shelf-prepared. Others combined the cataloging process and the acquisitions process, so that most materials were catalogued before they were ordered. Several of the campuses were considering joining on-line bibliographic services, such as OCLC, BIBNET, and SOLINET. Some state processing systems were in their infancy.

BOOK-, FICHE-, FILM-, AND COMPUTER-PRODUCED CATALOGS

Three single campuses and two three-campus districts had computer produced book catalogs. One of these employed a dual entry; there was one series with short entry, giving locations on the separate campuses, but including a register number where the full catalog card was reproduced photographically. Until the computerization of the card catalog, the separate libraries had no shelf lists of their holdings. Sometimes these catalogs were widely distributed; one campus printed 200 copies and distributed to each faculty member. Updating varied: monthly, quarterly, annually. One campus had both a card catalog and a computer catalog, and thought it might go with the book catalog only. One campus that used to have a book catalog had not updated it in two years and was planning to go back to the card catalog.

Another campus had a microfilm catalog produced by a commercial firm from punched tape. This campus used a conventional shelf list on cards as backup, and operated both simultaneously.

Four other campuses had catalogs on microfiche. These could be completely redone economically more often than book catalogs, but, of course, they required equipment for use.

Staff reported varying reactions to microform catalogs; some faculty resented it, other users liked it. One objection was that it required additional instruction to the reader in how to use it. None of the campuses having microform catalogs were observed to have reader-printers for convenience of the users; staff members agreed that reader printers would have provided complete, quick, and accurate bibliographic copy to facilitate searching and to eliminate handwritten notes.

COMPUTER APPLICATIONS

In addition to the circulation and book catalog applications already mentioned, learning resource departments were using computers for a variety of purposes: student rosters and faculty address lists; a variety of bibliographic lists; periodicals control; acquisitions and cataloging; budget and accounting control; detailed subject catalogs of photographic slide collections; audiovisual distribution of equipment and equipment inventory; on-line lookup of media materials by subject; and shelf lists. Computer use in instruction will be discussed in a later section.

Three campuses had very elaborate programs for computer control of periodicals. Aspects of these programs included: ordering, bid lists, direct orders, changing names; checking in and claiming; holdings listings (often merging unbound, bound and microfilm holdings); want lists; subject lists; source lists, and subscription schedules.

Computer programs in acquisition and cataloging included preorder cataloging; generation of the order; accounting reports by fund, type, requestor, vendor, and open items more than a specified date old; preparation of catalog cards or microfilm entry; spine labels, book cards, and pockets; and vendor files with names, addresses, specialties, etc.

Types of special lists included subject lists for faculty; lists of materials on reserve; music records by composer, performer, conventional and popular titles; college catalog acquisition lists with capability of producing request labels; company annual report request labels; ERIC documents lists; and software lists.

Chapter 10

DISTRIBUTION OF SOFTWARE AND MEDIA EQUIPMENT FOR CLASSROOM AND INDIVIDUAL USE

Community college learning resource staffs usually included a section whose responsibility was the scheduling, control, delivery, and setups of all media equipment and materials for classrooms; this section might or might not be the same unit which handled equipment and software used by individual students. In a few colleges the classroom distribution also included capability for closed circuit television distribution.

CLASSROOM DISTRIBUTION ORGANIZATION

A wide range of equipment was supplied for classroom use by most distribution sections of the learning resource departments, including: 16mm and 8mm projectors, slide projectors, overhead projectors, filmstrip projectors, opaque projectors, filmloop projectors, record players, tape recorders, video tape recorders and monitors, public address systems and cameras. Since volume of circulations was high, running into the hundreds, or on some large campuses, into several thousand per week, detailed scheduling systems were needed, and many distribution sections had a clerk whose sole responsibility was scheduling. Scheduling was usually done manually often using an hourly display board by means of multipart forms. These forms were utilized for confirming with the instructor, delivery, pickup, and location control. Obviously, advance notification was of great help; faculty varied in the amount of advance notice they gave.

In four campuses, the distribution department was responsible for the hardware, but the faculty member scheduled and picked up the software or film from some other department, such as the library. There were variations of at least four ways to get equipment into the classroom: a central pool of equipment which was transferred from there to the classroom, either with staff delivery, faculty member self pick up, student aid delivery; equipment closets in buildings scattered around the campus, with delivery or faculty checkout; or equipment deposited on extended loan to divisions, departments, or individual faculty with self scheduling if necessary.

Of the twenty-three learning resource departments that relied primarily on a central pool of equipment, twenty-two provided pickup and delivery service to and from the classroom; one required the faculty member to arrange his own pickup and delivery. This required a major commitment of time, seldom less than 70 man-hours per week, and often considerably more. Estimates of numbers of staff that would be pushing equipment simultaneously during a normal busy change of class time ranged from 1 regular staff and 3 students to 10 people. One campus did not use student aides for pickup and delivery, but had four full-time staff with this assignment. Another director said, "We get it there, on time, and we _all_ push equipment when necessary." Most directors thought that this service was essential if they wanted faculty to use the materials. One campus, threatened with a budget cut, discontinued pickup and delivery; all the faculty petitioned; the protest was so strong that the funding was restored in forty-eight hours. In addition to pickup and delivery, four campuses supplied operators; most campuses set up the software so that all the faculty member had to do was to start the machine.

In addition to the central equipment pool, seventeen campuses supplemented their pickup and delivery by permanent room assignments of heavily used equipment, by semester or extended loan to faculty or to departments, and by standing orders. Some pools to which faculty had keys were kept in each building. Lecture halls often had projection booths where equipment was locked in or bolted down; remote control from the lectern by the instructor saved having to schedule operators. Many campuses had overheads and screens in every teaching space; one campus had provided permanent placement of an overhead, a 16mm, a tape recorder, and a slide projector in 70% of its classrooms. On some campuses where theft rate was very low, they were moving more and more toward permanent installation, since they considered it a small risk in proportion to the greatly increased convenience and high savings. Some campuses were able to run their pickup and delivery systems on as few staff as they did because they took equipment as much as a half hour ahead and left it standing outside the door in the hall unattended; they considered it a calculated tradeoff of utility vs. convenience vs. theft risk. On four campuses most of the software was retained permanently in the departments.

Responsibility for special setups for public events, including community service use of campus facilities, was the responsibility of at least eleven of the media distribution sections. Sometimes outside groups brought their own equipment; however, sometimes they did not provide an operator. Sometimes operators for special academic events were charged back to departments. On two campuses the auditorium building had its own staff that did most of the routine setups, only calling in media specialists for the unusual.

16MM FILM RENTALS, COLLECTIONS, AND COOPERATIVES

Sixteen millimeter films were provided for classroom use on all campuses, but with varying administrative attitudes. Most media specialists were proud of their film collection and the efficiency of their rental operations. Three districts plus thirteen separate colleges, serving twenty-one campuses owned 16mm film collections. Four of these had 100 or fewer films; five had 200 to 400, three had 500 to 700, and four ranged from 960 to 3000 prints. Even those campuses with several hundred prints found that they still had to rent from 10 to 30% of their faculty requests. Some had a policy to buy; some to resist buying; "We could put as much as $100,000 a year into film and it would still not be enough; there is an inordinate amount of film use here." Distribution of 16mm film by closed circuit television was attempted on a few campuses, some with intercoms to the classrooms; but others had given it up because the faculty felt that the projected image was of much higher quality. One campus was developing a scheduling program based on punch card input.

At least seven campuses were very actively participating in film cooperatives, with other neighboring colleges, with a state higher education consortium, with city school systems, with major public libraries, and with a combined county cooperative.

EQUIPMENT

One director said, "I've gone all over the country and seen very expensive white elephant installations on a number of campuses. More and more, I have become convinced of the stupidity of <u>any</u> kind of large, fixed installation, particularly those with relatively limited purposes; inflexibility and inability to shift around and move with new technologies can kill you." Dial access, for example, loudly heralded a decade ago, was at the time of this study, "an embarrassment" on many campuses, according to the staff, although a few were still reporting excellent results: "We had very good luck with our dial access system, because we had the programs before we got the equipment, and a faculty momentum worked up to use. Our own staff installed it, which reduced the cost greatly and helped maintenance; we average 130,000 dials a year, and anything and everything in audio resources can be put on it, and is." Another very expensive installation was a gift to the college which the President had decided to accept in spite of the fact there was no software to put on it. Professionals and supportive staff were hired especially to assist faculty in making programs to fit the restrictions of the equipment, and the college had to supply personnel to run and maintain it. The equipment was so complicated that there was a significant amount of downtime. One of the supposed advantages of the system would have been that it was to be open all night seven days a week. Nevertheless, faculty and students had become so disenchanted with it that total enrollment was probably under 300. The same types of programs could have been supplied for individual carrell use on a checkout basis, with equipment costing about $300 per carrell.

Not only had campuses begun to sell or dismantle their dial access systems, but many were moving toward substitutes for studio television production. These campuses were seeking video systems that permitted more flexibility and could be moved to the locale of the action, rather than trying to bring everything to the studio. Language laboratories were being replaced by cassette players for home distribution. Some directors expressed their belief that video cassette and other development may have broad implications for future planning.

EQUIPMENT MAINTENANCE

Most media directors agreed that "Maintenance on equipment can make or break you." Prevention of downtime was a top objective. Campus repair crews operated at several levels: simple repairs of broken equipment, preventive maintenance, complicated repairs, and television production equipment repairs, which, particularly with color equipment, required a high level of training. Simple repairs were often handled by distribution and audiovisual technicians who had a limited repair bench in the distribution area. Sometimes elementary preventive maintenance, cleaning and checking were handled by students, although some engineers thought that this was very risky, and wasted more money than it saved.

The degree of sophisticated preventive maintenance varied with the skills of the maintenance crew available, but even more with the amount of personnel that was available. Where personnel shortages existed, preventive maintenance was sacrificed under the pressures of repairing equipment that was not operational. This crisis-centered repair of equipment and the lack of preventive maintenance might have cost more money for those campuses in the long run.

Several campuses had very systematized routines for preventive maintenance, often computerized. There was a detailed schedule by type of equipment and process; and each piece worked on was reported on a data processing form, which produced a weekly printout of activity and a log for each piece of equipment with a maintenance history. This history was, incidently, useful in evaluating brands and models for future purchase. In addition, this log, over the course of the year, provided data for patterned troubleshooting. Semester breaks were used to catch up on laboratory equipment and big installations. Each piece of equipment was coded when it was requisitioned; so that when it arrived, the inventory cards were already prepared, needing only the serial number and other information from the piece itself. The number could be painted on without delay, and the piece entered on computer. "Instructional Resources has the best inventory of anyone on campus."

The age of the system made a big difference in maintenance problems, availability of parts, and even whether service contracts or own staff were more satisfactory and economical, in terms of downtime. How much the maintenance crew could do also depended to some extent on whether the campus had enough equipment to pull several similar pieces off the line at the same time, to batch process them.

Several of the campuses stressed the economy of sending their maintenance staff regularly to factory training and service seminars, which were usually one to three days. This kept them up to date with the latest methods. One campus budgeted $800 annually for this type of training.

One director reported that 10% of inventory was the figure used in the district to defend maintenance budgets for personnel and parts, but not test equipment.

The availability of test equipment was critical in what could be done in house, for many types of equipment. Three directors expressed particular concern about the problems of test equipment for maintenance of television production equipment. One director thought TV ought to be contracted out because of the astronomical cost of expensive test equipment. In discussing contracting possibilities, another director said service contracts were not allowed because of state restrictions. Color television studio equipment particularly required scrupulous maintenance by highly trained crews, using very expensive equipment. Almost all campuses with color capability sent their crews to attend manufacturers' seminars regularly.

The Chief Engineer, who headed the maintenance crew, had a variety of responsibilities: training and supervision of maintenance and repair technicians; systems design, specification, and installation supervision; often consultation on the implementation of educational specifications, especially technical aspects; equipment specification, testing, and design. His background ranged from AA degree to post Masters, and often included state Professional Engineers' license and First Class Federal Communications Commission Broadcast license.

Evaluations of the quality of equipment maintenance done on each campus was mixed. About one-third of the directors thought their maintenance was not adequate, usually because the staff was too small, occasionally because it was not sufficiently well trained. About a third thought it was about adequate, but even some of them said the same level of maintenance would not be adequate in a short time because the equipment was aging. A third thought their maintenance was superb, top notch, and more than paying its way.

LEARNING LABORATORIES

Most campuses had developed various kinds of learning laboratories where materials, often both print and non-print, and equipment were available to students. These materials might be supplementary to the classroom, reinforcing, remedial, or might be intended for auto-tutorial, or independent learning. Self-instruction study stations might employ the full range of AV equipment used for classroom media presentations, plus programmed instruction materials, and various types of self-instructional equipment such as autotutors, testing devices, re-record equipment, and reading improvement equipment.

Types of software used in laboratory situations included: tapes, filmstrips (with and without sound), slide/tape syncronizations, film-loops, discs, slide sets, audiscan, autotutor, simulated games, programmed books, transparency sets, models, maps, continuous reader and scanner programs, dictation tapes, independent study courses, scrambled books, teaching machine programs, scripts, 16mm films, videotapes, cassettes, 8mm films, computer aided instruction programs, microfilm and microfiche, and occasionally realia.

The advantages often mentioned, and included in student brochures of individual instructional learning laboratory packages were: availability of a variety of materials, various paths to learning, differing levels of difficulty or assumed background and preparation, different formats for varying tastes. It was usually stressed that the student could proceed independently, free from competition, and entirely at his own speed, establishing his own schedule. It was also noted that specific effectiveness of the various units could be tested separately and improvements made where students did not comprehend; that educational objectives could be very specifically spelled out, for both the student and the instructor; and that the package provided the student with everything he needed to satisfy the objectives. Some directors said that effective instruction was a student's right; he grew up in a mediated world, and ought to be able to expect no less from the environment responsible for having the major impact on his adult activity and behavior.

Sometimes there was a centralized, consolidated learning laboratory covering a variety of subjects; this might have been in the Learning Resource Center, the Library, or in one of the other academic buildings. This consolidated installation was usually administered by the audiovisual staff, where the library staff was separate, but in a few instances it was administered by the librarians. In addition to, or instead of, the consolidated lab, there might have been one or more special subject labs for a particular discipline.

Departmental labs covered a wide range of the curriculum. Among the types mentioned were:

Accounting 4
Automobile mechanics 1
Aviation and flight simulation 1
Anatomy and physiology 1
Art 3

Biology 12
Business 3

Chemistry 6
Court reporting 1

Data processing 4
Dental hygiene 1
Drafting 2

Economics 1
Education 1
Engineering 2
English 4

Fire Science 1

Health Science, Allied Health 3
History 1

Language lab 11
Logic 1

Mathematics 16
Management technology 1
Music 5

Nursing 6

Optometry 1

Physical education 2
Physics 2
Psychology 2

Radiology 2
Reading 8

Science, biological 1	Term papers 1
Science physical 3	
Secretarial science 4	Writing 3
Speech 3	

Campuses reported widely varying success with student use of the learning laboratories. Some reported that usage was growing dramatically, at about 150% a year. Another director's report to his administration stated, "It is hoped that the latest revision will cut down somewhat on this attrition problem. However, an informal survey of other independent study programs on campuses revealed that large attrition rates seem to be an inherent problem in programs of this type." Comprehensive measurements of student usage of the learning laboratories were available from only four campuses. Method of measurement differed markedly, and meaningful comparisons probably would not have been possible even if a larger number had been available. The total usage in these four campuses ranged from 8,732 to 57,074.

While learning resource personnel were almost always responsible for staffing, maintenance, scheduling, and equipping the consolidated labs, their responsibility toward the departmental labs varied. Infrequently they were responsible for staffing, but usually the staffing was provided by the academic departments. Usually the media staff were held responsible for maintaining the equipment and often for helping produce materials for the lab. Particularly, they were usually involved in design of the lab, specifying equipment, installing, or supervising installation. Who paid for the equipment varied; sometimes the academic department, the learning resource department, or the media department received a grant for the installation. Location of the department labs was often justified on the basis that it needed to be near some other teaching resource; for example, the biology auto-tutorial laboratory was usually located adjacent to the regular biology laboratory.

Learning resource administrators on many campuses had had expressions of academic ambivalence toward labs: the experience of academic departments wanting labs, starting them in the learning center, wanting to move them to their own building, not being willing to provide adequate staffing, wanting to get rid of them back to the learning resource center, and then in a few years wanting them back again. Most LRC administrators were showing a deliberate tendency to drag their feet on the planning of a new lab until the value to the instructional program was proved in test trials within the learning center or elsewhere. Most administrators also wanted careful analysis of the effectiveness of the content and format of the software packages to be used in these labs. "The college has a tremendous capital investment in the learning laboratories," was an often expressed sentiment. Departments usually justified learning laborities by enrollment.

INDIVIDUAL STUDENT USE OF MEDIA MATERIALS

There were very mixed attitudes from campus to campus on independent individual student use of visual materials, films, slides, loops, transparencies, videotapes, etc. Some campuses made almost no provision at all for individual student viewing; other campuses catalogued every thing that the school bought or made, and everything was accessible to students for individual viewing except when it was scheduled for showing in a class. Individual student use of audio materials was somewhat better provided for.

More than half the campuses made a very sharp and strong distinction between those materials bought or produced for the faculty for use in class and those materials bought or produced for learning packages for individual use by the students. Often these materials were treated entirely separately both in organization and handling, and particularly in student accessibility. In about one third of the campuses, materials bought or made for classroom use were unavailable for use by students on an individual basis. Some directors acknowledged that individual students might benefit from being able to see materials shown in classes they had missed, or to review materials they did not fully comprehend. Nevertheless, they stated that they were not geared to handle this type of student request, that they couldn't handle the number of students who might want to use this service if available, that they didn't have enough space, equipment, or enough personnel to handle setups for individual students, that they didn't think it was desirable to let students browse in the materials faculty would want to show them, that the school's philosophy did not encourage this type of exploration by the students, and that they deliberately did not let the students know how much or what materials they had. Some directors who did not permit student access wished they were able to; some were hoping to be able to expand in this direction when construction of additional facilities permitted; one hoped he would be able to combine the classroom collection and the learning lab collections into a single unit with ready access to all. At least five of these campuses did permit students to use classroom materials if they brought written permission from their instructors, or if the instructor was willing to come with the students to use it jointly, or if the instructor would sign it out for use by the student in the faculty member's office.

Slightly less than a third of the campuses permitted ready, on-demand student access to some of the classroom materials, but not to others. The most commonly restricted types of materials were 16mm films and videotapes. Some directors felt that these very expensive materials were too perishable to permit individual use. "A 16mm film wears out in 200 showings; we just can't afford it." Some directors said that they did not have preview rooms that students could use, and that they thought equipment for individual use in lighted rooms was unsatisfactory, and they did not feel commitment of space for light, sound, and ventilation control would be justified. "Some of our students would do nothing all day long except lie around looking at films."

In slightly more than a third of the campuses students had ready access for use in the learning center to all materials, regardless of whether they had originally been bought for classroom use. "Everything we've got they can use--and pretty regularly do." "We've got all this stuff; why have it gathering dust; put your mouth where your money is." Another campus would not only let students use whatever they owned, but would rent materials for individual student use on request. Another director said, "We have to re-teach them that equipment and software are for _them_, too, not just for faculty."

Of these, six campuses permitted students to borrow for home use in addition to cassettes, some other types of software. Although these types did not generally include 16mm or videotapes, on one campus, even these were circulated for home use, although somewhat restricted, if material had not been scheduled the next day for class use. One campus had a special extension service for students taking external degrees; they sent the software to the students. Circulation of equipment to students for their own use included a wide variety of projection and playback equipment in three campuses, including still and motion picture cameras; one campus even lent portable video production equipment to students for their independent use.

INSTRUCTING THE STUDENTS IN USE OF MEDIA MATERIALS

Most of the campuses relied primarily on the faculty to tell the students what was available in media materials and to get them to use it. The selection of materials for the media collection was almost universally course oriented; much of the selection had been done by the faculty, or in consultation with them. Faculty told the students what was available, or the students could ask the learning laboratories assistants who were pretty familiar with the collection. One campus mentioned that students often got to know about media materials through the student newspaper. Another said that the lab itself attracted the curious, and the students would often hear of materials from word of mouth. Audiovisual directors in five campuses thought that the reference librarians knew very little about the media collection, and that there was not much likelihood that they would suggest that students use specific materials in it. In contrast, seven AV directors thought that the reference staff were media conscious, did pretty well know the AV collection and did promote the use of non-print as well as print materials.

There was concern expressed on some campuses for improving the instruction of students in how to use equipment. Some had had considerable experience with equipment in high school; others lacked confidence. One AV director did equipment "hands-on" orientation with each class that was going to be given lab assignments; "I try to make it enjoyable."

CATALOGING OF AUDIOVISUAL MATERIALS

One of the complex problems was insuring that faculty knew both for their own class use, and for referring their students for individual use, what the full range of available resources in their areas were, especially as collections grow to significant sizes. This was especially significant since the faculty was largely responsible for student awareness of and motivation toward using media.

Most campuses that had film collections issued lists of these films, primarily to faculty. These lists sometimes had extensive annotations, and subject indexes. Sometimes they were alphabetical by title, sometimes by some classification scheme, sometimes arranged by department. Some of these were revised annually, with interim supplements, some every two years, some were even older. In addition to the 16mm film published lists, three campuses had issued lists of video tape one of audio tape two of phonodiscs, and three had very elaborate indexes produced by computer analysis of their slide collections. One campus had made no attempt to catalog its slides, but put them into plastic holders of notebook size, then photographed each sheet to use as a microfiche index to the slide collection.

In addition to these lists, seven campuses had issued comprehensive lists of all audiovisual materials, regardless of format. On one campus students had access to the phonodisc portion of the comprehensive catalog, but the rest of it was kept behind the desk for faculty use only. One other media department had a card file of its holdings. On one campus where most of the software was housed in department offices, the librarian had obtained lists of these holdings on file in the library.

In the card catalog or book catalog seventeen campuses had included cataloging for all software integrated with the books and print material. Most of them attempted to have as high standards for media cataloging as for print material. The classification system, however, was sometimes totally different. Nevertheless, several media directors expressed concern that they believed that a substantial part of the total college holdings had never been catalogued; their estimates of the proportion of uncatalogued holdings ranged from 25% to 70% of the total collection.

Five campuses made no attempt at this time to catalog audiovisual materials.

Some campuses that regularly catalogued all purchased audiovisual materials did not catalog materials that were locally produced. Two reasons for this were that this material was constantly being revised and changed; and that it was very difficult to obtain complete bibliographic information from the production department or the faculty member who made the item.

One campus had on-line capability for subject lookup of media materials.

STUDENT PRODUCTION OF MEDIA MATERIALS, AND STUDENT COURSES

In addition to offering credit courses, discussed below, in production and use of media, eleven campuses had special facilities and provided advisory and other assistance to students in doing their own independent production of audiovisual materials. Sometimes these materials were related to courses they were taking and would be presented by them in class, sometimes they were not related to their course programs. In several schools the English department would accept such a production in place of term papers. Production facilities for students often included a student operated darkroom and in four cases, a black and white television studio. Some of the campus bookstores stocked supplies for this use. One school had an independent production room for students and faculty, including audio, photography, and graphics capability. Staff were available to tell students how to make their projects and sometimes to give them help all the way down the line. One school had a regular media workshop for students and a full time person to help them. "We threw open the doors the last part of last semester, and had 18; now it's a fully open door and we expect 180." One school had a slide collection especially for the use of students to incorporate into their productions; it started as an accident, was too useful to discard, and was then regularly augmented.

Although some of the campuses which offered credit courses in production or utilization of various media had a separate instructional faculty independent of the learning resource staff, several of the learning resource staff did teach credit courses. These courses included one equipment course; one general production and one media utilization course particularly geared toward special education, social work and child development specialists; television courses. (Six campuses offered these, one of which is at night in continuing education for the community.) Two campuses had two year programs in Media Technology. Under the Library Services Act, one campus had workshops each May in each district with on-site visits.

COMPUTER AIDED INSTRUCTION

At least eleven campuses were becoming involved to some extent in the application of computers in instruction, although CAI was not yet operational in three of them, and only one of the others offered more than five courses in which CAI was employed. CAI was under a variety of academic departments, including Mathematics, Data Processing, and Business, and in one case had its own staff directly under the Dean of Instruction. One campus was part of a community college district that had developed over eighty programs running under CAI from a central installation. A district coordinator spent one day a week on each campus. The campus visited had 8 terminals on campus, six of which were in the learning resource center; these terminals averaged about 4 hours per day usage.

Three campuses were very actively involved in CMI--Computer Managed Instruction--especially in grading student tests, evaluating results for the instructor, and charting the student's progress through the course. Using this approach in auto-tutorial biology, 528 students were being supervised by only 3 faculty. Weekly testing was done on mark sense cards, the computer took care of all record keeping, and printed out in full to faculty total activity. Problems in comprehension of specific material were more readily apparent than with conventional scoring. There were conferences between faculty and students and small groups assemblies for feedback. The Mathematics auto-tutorial was going to a similar approach. Terminals for on-line testing were being planned. Another campus was developing programs to use the computer to reduce attrition and failure rate by identifying patterns in such variables as attendance and test scores.

TESTING PROGRAMS

Four learning resource departments were involved in administering testing programs within the LRC building. Three of these test centers handled academic testing only; the fourth was also involved in diagnostic testing for entering students, personal and personality testing, and vocational testing for the community. By using the test centers, the college avoided taking up class time with testing; students came at their convenience, the tests were scored mechanically, and the tabulated results returned to the instructor. One LRC was very actively developing test review packages to help students get better scores. Two other campuses did not use a testing center to administer tests, but did assign to the learning resource department the running of the mechanical test scoring machinery. Three campuses reported very satisfactory performances from their test scoring machinery, with almost no downtime One campus had a special project involving the LRC in video tape testing of student skills performance.

Chapter 11

PRODUCTION OF AUDIOVISUAL MATERIALS

All twenty-seven campuses were involved to some extent in production of audiovisual materials, although they varied widely in production capability, quantities of production, and media most often employed. Complete and detailed production statistics were available from five campuses, and some statistics from several others; nevertheless, methods of reporting quantities varied sufficiently as to make comparative analysis impossible or computations of measures of central tendency questionable. Numbers were sometimes reported as numbers of jobs (and a job might be several hundred items), sometimes in quantities produced: reels, prints, feet of film, etc. The five comprehensive reports ranged in total numbers from about 400 jobs to over 40,000 items. The five colleges themselves in no case added their reports to get totals, since this would have resulted in the absurdity of adding feet to reels to minutes, etc. Four campuses stated that they had very limited production capability; here modesty and perspective in self-assessment entered the discussion, because what one director might consider very limited, another might have considered quite adequate.

One or more campuses reported production capability for each of the following types of media:

- Graphic Arts
  - Transparencies
    - Thermo
    - Diazo
    - Photomodifiers
    - Color lifts
- Filmmaking, color, B/W
  - 16mm
    - Silent
    - Sound

Graphic arts (continued)
- Ditto masters
- Spirit masters
- Offset masters
- Metal Plates for duplicating
- Paper copies
- Signs
  - Printed
  - Hand lettered
- Posters
- Original artwork & design
  - Camera ready art
- Lamination
- Dry mounting

Photography
- Slides (2x2)
  - Copy
  - Duplication
  - Original
- Negatives
  - 8x10
  - 4x5
  - Rolls
- Prints
  - B/W
  - Color
- Polaroid
  - B/W
  - Color
- ID pictures
- Filmstrips

Filmmaking (continued)
- Super 8
  - Reels
    - Silent
    - Sound
  - Filmloops
    - Silent
    - Sound

Audio
- Original recordings
  - Reel
  - Cassette
  - Sync
- Duplication
  - Reel-to-reel
  - Cassette
- Record-to-tape transfer
- 16mm sound transfer
- Audio mix

Television, recordings
- Color, B/W
  - Original
    - Studio
    - Location
  - Duplication
    - Off air
    - Tape-to-tape

Every campus had the capability of making 2x2 slides. The quantity of slides reported to have been produced per year ranged from 200 to 150,000 per campus; the median was about 11,000. These slides were used in sets, with and without narration. The next most common form of production was audio cassette, with a substantial amount of reel-to-reel audio taping still being done. The median number of cassettes being produced was about 5,000. The next most common form was transparencies for overhead projection, with a median per year of approximately 2,000 per campus.

Seven campuses had active cinematography sections. Two regularly filmed intercollegiate athletic events. One campus produced 16mm films for sale on a rotating fund basis. Originally, this LRC had decided on a major production effort, and had gone to the Board of Trustees to underwrite it.

From the sales, rentals, and preview fees accruing from that film, they retained a production fund to use for the next one; thus their films have paid for themselves.

Production was expensive not only because of the costs of equipment, raw stock and processing, but also because of the amount of labor involved. Some directors estimated that a simple slide presentation might have required an average of three hours preparation for every minute on the screen. Complex productions, especially those multimedia productions requiring the synchronization of several media, might have required much longer. Production coordinators had several responsibilities: to keep the materials flowing, to coordinate the efforts of the individuals producing the components of the package, and to coordinate its assemblance. Detailed scheduling boards were sometimes employed, with due date promised to the faculty, and assignments for each production unit. Establishment of priorities for production sometimes became a touchy issue, since almost no one's capabilities were underutilized in production departments. "We talk to the faculty, and try to handle everything, but we may have to juggle and negotiate due dates." Directors stressed the importance of giving faculty realistic deadlines. Major production requests usually involved a formal application, which was sometimes screened by committees or deans.

Many multi-campus districts were finding that having a central production facility with expensive equipment didn't really work as anticipated. The directors cited this major factor: the resistance of faculty to keep traveling to the district office for their production needs. This major facility, therefore, which was designed to serve the whole district, often wound up doing most of its work for the campus on which it was located, and very little for the others. Where there was more than one campus, directors assessed from experience, that each must have its own basic production facility.

There was one exception to this: cinematography capability, some thought, should not be duplicated on each campus.

In deciding on production format, many directors tried to avoid media for its own sake, by examining the content of the message to be taught, and then deciding whether color, motion or synchronized sound was necessary. Finally, they then selected the medium that represented the most conservative expenditure which would adequately get the message across. High enrollment courses were cost effective for mediation; single section courses were not, usually. Slides, where motion was not required, were considered to be interchangeable, easily updated, inexpensive, and easy to duplicate without loss of quality. Several campuses had detailed production handbooks for use with staff of the LRC and the faculty, including guidelines for man-hour estimates in graphics and charts of work flow.

One campus staff said its institution did not always look for quality, but was more committed to quantity and immediacy. Another said, "We _try_; the staff has the expertise, but we have severe equipment limitations; quality is being phased in gradually." The overwhelming majority felt strongly that the Learning Resource department and the campus in general had a strong commitment to professional quality of production. "You have a sophisticated audience, accustomed from infancy to professional quality and demanding it; education is light years beind commercial TV. If you aren't willing to spend a lot of money, don't get in the act." "High quality is the only educationally sound approach; poor quality distracts; if the quality is good to begin with, it will last longer, and result in savings in the long run." "It's essential that productions get and keep attention, be entertaining and be interesting--and that isn't easy or inexpensive."

Production directors admitted that they often came in conflict with faculty about quality in production, and had to use tact and persuasion to counter faculty impatience and time restrictions. "Our quality is always increasing; we've made a big change over our four years, educating the faculty to what quality to expect." Other directors said they would not let faculty use homemade materials; whatever faculty wanted to use had to be reviewed for quality by a professional production person, who might require that it be done over if possible, although some compromises were inevitable. "We're accused of rigidity, at times, but our commitment to quality control has proved its effectiveness."

A few production directors thought they had very generous space for production, but most were crowded because of the variety and complexity of their activities; "We're spilling out all over the place." Some campuses had almost no space specifically allocated to production, which had to share corners with other activities. Others had very extensive production facilities, including:

Photography labs

Still photography studios

Darkrooms, print rooms and finishing rooms

Audio studios and control rooms

Storage space of all kinds

Engineering, maintenance and repair

TV studios and control rooms

Closed circuit TV distribution rooms

TV reproduction

Previewing and conference rooms

Staff office space

Prop rooms

Loading docks and receiving rooms

Carpentry shops and model shops

Graphics studios

Print Shops

Cinematography studios

The print shop was under the administration of the Learning Resources department in three campuses. Two others would like to have it, "but haven't won the battle." Others did not have it, did not want it, and were fighting not to be stuck with it; "That print shop does 5,000,000 copies a year, and everything's a headache."

Television production capability ranged from portable half-inch helical scan equipment, to non-broadcast quality black and white helical scan studio equipment, to broadcast quality (FCC standards) color quadruplex equipment. Eleven campuses had at least some (some still in installation stages) capability for closed circuit cable television distribution to various points around the campus, and a few multicampus colleges were using microwave hookups to transmit between campuses. Three campuses had television production vans equipped with top quality equipment that could be backed up to instructional buildings all over the campus for broadcast quality on-site production.

While some campuses regularly checked out Porta-pak equipment to be operated by faculty, or even students, most campuses tried to supply a cameraman whenever video taping was being done; "The instructor's job is to perform, to stimulate students, to be creative, and to direct; if he has to mind the camera too, a lot of the benefit is lost." For studio work, most campuses generally scheduled a crew of five for any video taping: two cameramen (who might be well-trained students), a producer/director, an engineer, and perhaps a third cameraman or an audio man, depending on the needs of the production.

Amount of use of television in class instruction varied from discipline to discipline, but on one campus, "Almost every course uses at least some video taping" Disciplines which were heavily dependent on video taping for instruction included: speech, nursing, allied health, especially dentistry, physical education, and theater. Taping had proved its effectiveness not only in evaluating student performance, including self-evaluation, and in immediate reinforcement; but it had also been used for faculty self evaluation in the improvement of their teaching. One campus had a special project of video taping live fires in the area for their fire science program.

On most campuses, video taping was only one of the means used to reinforce instruction; they did not video tape whole courses. However, a few entire courses had been made and marketed; some were distributed by live broadcast to the community. Marketability was a factor that many directors kept in mind when considering productions.

In addition to media production for instruction, including classroom use and individual use by students, many production departments also did work primarily intended for administration, public relations, recruitment, and staff training at the college. This type activity might have included the college bulletin (catalog), brochures, posters and signs, and photographing and recording special events. Since the latter type of work tended to crowd out instructional production when staff were short-handed ("the president and deans always come first"), the ratio of non-instructional production was a concern to many media directors. The range in proportion varied from none or almost to no non-instruction related production (because the college had a separate public relations department) to 10% instruction, 15% instructionally related (extracurricular activities, student productions, student recruiting), 75% public relations and administration. The median was probably about 40%-20%-40%.

Responsibilities of the learning resource staff to instructional design and development, included helping faculty in designing or redesigning instruction through systematic planning and sequence, defining and clarifying their instructional objectives, and designing the media to present content as effectively and efficiently as possible. This instructional design and development aspect, however, varied widely both in staff attitude and practice.

In some campuses there was little if any of this type of activity; in others it was a major effort.

Some learning resource staff felt strongly that this was not their responsibility, and that to attempt it would be to get into a hornet's nest. "I don't hassle the faculty about content, and they don't hassle me about format. The faculty are responsible for the message; they are the subject specialists. I am the media specialist; given the message, it's my job to get it across. They may come in thinking they know what medium they want; we discuss it; if necessary, I get arbitrary."

Other staff, although they might have thought that much more help was needed by faculty, recognized the intensity of faculty jealousy of their prerogatives, and therefore, made haste slowly and cautiously in advising, suggesting, informal conferences, and discussion. It was often difficult even to get faculty to admit that they might have been having instructional problems and needed help.

On other campuses, there were special staff members whose full responsibility was increasing the efficiency of instruction and instructional presentations. They conferred with faculty on improvement of objectives; effectiveness of idea design and content; and efficiency of format. In addition, they had a great deal of leeway in interaction with faculty in message development. They discussed available options and refined exactly what the faculty member wanted to do. They were especially trained in the writing of instructional modules. After content had been decided on, the production staff was brought in to discuss format.

Seven campuses said they had no release time or payment for salaries of faculty working with learning resource staff in the development of instructional packages. Seventeen campuses said they had some form of release time or payment, although some of them felt it was inadequate. Two campuses had substantial lump sums of money for special release projects; faculty interested in projects applied annually for these funds for major production efforts. The project proposals were reviewed by a committee, which usually included a member of the earning esource staff. The committee would split the funds and award the money to the outstanding plans. Two districts said that their district had set aside 2% of the instructional budget for instructional development by faculty, primarily released time. Some learning resource staff, and some college administrations, felt that there had been significant abuses of the release time system, and that there were few usable results coming out of the programs. Other colleges had dealt with this sore point by requiring specific contracts for special projects, paying some initial production money, but not paying the faculty until completion and delivery of the material. Some faculty resisted production because they feared that it would be used to reduce or replace faculty. Other faculty were very concerned about the right to copyright and market what they had produced; one campus had developed its own policy for the faculty ownership of locally produced materials, others had no policy or were using adaptations of the policy developed by the University of Michigan. There was much discussion about whether or not faculty should be charged back for the materials and labor of the learning resource staff used in the development of the package; some LRC staffs felt that they had contributed the lion's share of the value of the production, and that the instructor's contribution had been minimal. Some colleges charged back; others did not.

CONCLUSION

At the time of this survey, activities in learning resource departments of large community colleges were almost overwhelming in their variety.

It is hoped that in a future outgrowth of this study, data gathering instruments can be devised which will provide consistent means of getting truly comparable data on this range of activities, and a broad, representative, across-the-board sample used for obtaining information about campuses of all sizes and budgets. Valid and reliable means of measuring are essential before meaningful standards can be written.

The implications and experiences gained in community college learning resource centers have broad application to both elementary and secondary schools and to all types of institutions of higher education. Both faculty and learning resource staffs would agree that in utilization of learning resources in higher education, community colleges are definitely where the action is.

Appendix A

TENTATIVE INTERVIEW SCHEDULE

DIRECTOR OR ASSOCIATE DIRECTOR:

1. Major responsibilities of the department. Relationship of other departments to Library and Learning Resource Center.

2. Budget: 5 yr. trend; possible future.
   Organization, categories. Flexibility?
   How developed: staff, faculty, administrative input.

3. Capital budget, including construction and alterations. Bidding, contracts.

4. Part of state/county/city system? Multi-unit campuses? How related.
   Centralized functions? Amount of autonomy?

5. What kinds of things charged to other departments? How much LLRC control?

6. Major projects supported by special grants? Their future?

7. Staff organization. Ratio of salaries to rest of the budget. Professional to clerical ratio. Is clerical staff adequate?

8. Purchasing. How organized, controlled. How much done outside the dept.?

9. Where are they going: accomplishments, objectives, goals.

MEDIA UTILIZATION ADMINISTRATOR:

1. Advisement to students and faculty on use. Accessibility. Catalogs.

2. Mediation of instruction. Development. Release time. Administrative support.

MEDIA PRODUCTION COORDINATOR:

1. Budget for rawstock, film, tape, supplies, etc. Equipment. Commercially or other preproduced software. 16mm films.

2. Facilities.

3. Staff. Relationship to demand.

4. What proportion of staff and budget going into non-instructional projects like college publicity, print shop, maintenance, etc.

REFERENCE AND INFORMATION ADMINISTRATOR:

1. Activities and usage.

2. Who selects materials. Role of faculty, LRC staff. Previews.

COMPUTER EXPERT

1. How used? Who pays for it? On/off line. Programming. Who handles input/output? Campus computer.

CIRCULATION ADMINISTRATOR.

1. Control points. Hours open. Staff. Physical layout of building.

2. Open or closed stacks for: books, reserves, periodicals, 16mm films, other software; restrictions on student use.

3. Circulation usage. Regular, reserve, periodicals, film, audio, other software, in house, photocopy, including microprinter.
By type of borrower.
Any statistics on proportion of the collection used?

CLASSROOM DISTRIBUTION ADMINISTRATOR.

1. How handled? Amount of staff, student aids. Scheduling.
Pickup and delivery.

PERIODICALS:

1. How handled? Are they satisfied? Checking in, circulation, cataloging, binding.

APPENDIX B

PRODUCTION__ Please indicate Department responsible, and number of FTE staff.

	Library Learning Res. Center (combined)	Learning Resource Center (separate)	Other (Please specify)	Staff		
				Professional	Semi- or Tech. Asst.	Other
Slides						
Overhead transparencies .						
Graphics						
Motion pictures						
Audio recordings						
Radio						
Studio television						
Non-studio television . .						
Printing and duplicating .						
Other: ____________						
____________						
____________						

What department in your college is responsible for:

	Library and Learning Res. Center	Learning Res. Center, if separate	Other (please specify)
INSTRUCTION			
Individual student instruction and guidance in:			
Use of print materials	______	______	______
Use of non-print materials	______	______	______
Classroom instruction of students:			
Use of print materials	______	______	______
Use of non-print materials	______	______	______
Formal courses:			
For faculty:			
Print materials, bibliography	______	______	______
Non-print materials			
Use	______	______	______
Production	______	______	______
For students:			
Print, bibliography.	______	______	______
Non-print (indicate types)	______	______	______
Faculty workships, seminars, etc.			
Print	______	______	______
Non-print	______	______	______
INSTRUCTIONAL DEVELOPMENT	______	______	______
Design of mediated instruction	______	______	______
CLASSROOM DISTRIBUTION OF AV EQUIPMENT, MATERIALS .	______	______	______
LANGUAGE LABORATORY, MUSIC LABORATORY	______	______	______
MAINTENANCE OF EQUIPMENT	______	______	______
TESTING CENTER	______	______	______
OTHER: ______________________	______	______	______

APPENDIX D

How many of your staff have graduate training in both print and non-print media:

At least 5th year in both (two degrees)______________.
Combined degree in both (one degree)______________.
Fifth year degree in one, at least 15 graduate points in the other ______________.
Fifth year degree in one, some graduate points in the other______________.

Please indicate the approximate number of full-time equivalent staff that are engaged in each of the following types of activities:

	Professional	Semi-, Para-professional, Technical Assistants	Supportive staff, incl secretaries, clerical
Administration	________	________	________
Selection of materials	________	________	________
Acquisition, purchasing	________	________	________
Cataloging	________	________	________
Media utilization	________	________	________
Reference and information	________	________	________
Circulation, print materials . . .	________	________	________
Circulation, non-print matls	________	________	________
Class room distribution of AV equipment and materials . .	________	________	________
Production of materials	________	________	________
Engineering and maintenance . . .	________	________	________
Other: ________________	________	________	________
________________	________	________	________
TOTAL STAFF (FTE)	________	________	________